Mary—

Greetings f[...]

Hartford

12 September '93

Erich + Shirley

*H*erbs
for all
*S*easons

Herbs
for all
Seasons

ROSEMARY HEMPHILL

VIKING

For

Margaret Davis, MBE
in appreciation of her kind
encouragement at the start of our
herb and spice venture

VIKING
Published by the Penguin Group
Penguin Books USA Inc., 375 Hudson Street,
New York, New York 10014, U.S.A.
Penguin Books Ltd, 27 Wrights Lane, London W8 5TZ, England
Penguin Books Australia Ltd, Ringwood, Victoria, Australia
Penguin Books Canada Ltd, 10 Alcorn Avenue,
Toronto, Ontario, Canada M4V 3B2
Penguin Books (N.Z.) Ltd, 182–190 Wairau Road, Auckland 10, New Zealand

Penguin Books Ltd, Registered Offices: Harmondsworth, Middlesex, England

First American Edition
Published in 1993 by Viking Penguin, a division of Penguin Books USA Inc.

1 3 5 7 9 10 8 6 4 2

A NOTE TO THE READER
Some herbs, if misused, can be harmful. This book is not a medical reference
book. The advice it contains is general, not specific, and neither the author nor
the publishers can be held responsible for any adverse reactions to any use of
herbs mentioned herein.

Black-and-white illustrations by Claire Simpson
Color illustrations and cover art by Skye Rogers

Page vi constitutes an extension of this copyright page.

ISBN 0-670-85041-1
CIP data available

Printed in Hong Kong
Set in Times

Contents

Acknowledgments for Copyright Material

Acknowledgments and thanks are due to the following publishers and authors for permission to use copyright material:

To Barrie & Jenkins for the recipe for Dandelion Wine from *Home-made Wines and Liqueurs* by Ambrose Heath.

To Chatto & Windus for the recipe for Nasturtium Salad from *The Gentle Art of Cookery* by Mrs Leyel and Olga Hartley.

To Faber and Faber for four recipes from *A Calendar of Country Recipes* by Nell Heaton, namely Crabapple and Rowan Jelly; Sorrel Omelette; Elderberry Wine; Rose-hip Syrup.

To the executors of the estate of Mrs C. F. Leyel for the recipe for A Liver and Kidney Mixture from *A Modern Herbal* by Mrs M. Grieve.

To the executor of the estate of E. S. Rohde for the recipe for a Mixture for a Sore Throat or Cough from *A Garden of Herbs* by Eleanour Sinclair Rohde.

To Phoenix House Ltd for two recipes from *A Herbal of All Sorts* by Geoffrey Grigson, namely Elder Milk; Comfrey Fritters.

To the National Federation of Women's Institutes, England, for several recipes from *Lotions and Potions*, namely A Lavender Bottle; Balm Tea for Strengthening the Memory; Elizabethan or Elderberry Rob; Elderflower Ointment; A Tonic and Restorative for the Hair; A Mixture to Relieve a Heavy Cold; A Liniment for Bronchitis.

Some thoughts on food for health and enjoyment

This book contains many recipes for healthy living but does not follow any one kind of diet. The aim is for well-balanced eating comprising as many wholesome foods as possible: honey and raw sugar; unrefined flours and breads made from unrefined flours; wheat germ; fresh lean meats, fresh poultry and fish; seeds and nuts; fresh vegetables and fruits, if possible grown organically or bio-dynamically and untouched by poisonous sprays; unsaturated or cold-pressed vegetable oils; kelp; herb or vegetable salt or sea salt; eggs; dairy foods that have undergone a natural type of processing, such as yoghurt, cottage cheese, block cheese and buttermilk ... It is a personal choice whether cream is eaten, whether to use butter or margarine, or to substitute dehydrated skimmed milk (which is very nourishing) for fresh whole milk.

The herbs, flowers, berries and fruits with which this book is concerned are arranged according to their seasons, and there are recipes for their use as simple remedies as well as in cooking. It becomes clear to the interested researcher that claims concerning the healing power of herbs are well founded: this is shown in the writings of physicians and herbalists from past centuries to the present day, as well as in one's own experience. These humble plants possess a special alchemy that transforms various elements into potent forces that pervade their substance. There is a widely held belief that herbs of one kind or another can heal the troubles of any part of the body: for instance, rosemary helps the functions of the head, sage those of the throat and mouth. Even more specifically—as Mrs Leyel says in *The Truth About Herbs*—a herb can influence a particular organ, a particular part of an organ, or even a particular nerve.

As well as having healing qualitites, herbs and spices enliven food and aid the digestion. Wholesome aromas and natural flavours arouse the senses of smell and taste, promoting the healthy flow of digestive juices and enabling the body to gain the greatest possible nutriment from food.

Herbs are not hard to grow, even if you have no garden and live in a flat*. However, dried herbs are excellent in cooking provided they have been properly dried and are kept stored in closed containers to seal in their flavour and preserve their colour. The quantites given in the recipes in this book are for fresh herbs. With dried herbs, it is usually necessary to measure half to one-third less, depending on the strength of flavour wished for. When herbs are dried carefully, only the watery element evaporates, not the essential oils, which become concentrated and therefore stronger. (There are one or two exceptions, which will be referred to as we come to them.)

* I have written about this in *Fragrance and Flavour* and in *The Penguin Book of Herbs and Spices*.

Spring

SPICY FINES HERBS
chervil chives parsley,

NOURISHING POT HERBS
dandelion borage lovage sorrel

A BOUQUET OF FLOWERS FOR
FRAGRANCE AND HEALTH
iris roses lavendar violets

It was a lover and his lass,
With a hey, and a ho, and a hey nonino,
That o'er the green corn-field did pass,
In the spring time, the only pretty ring time,
When birds do sing, hey ding a ding, ding:
Sweet lovers love the spring.

WILLIAM SHAKESPEARE, As You Like It, 5, III

Spring in the world of Nature means reawakened activity, new life, and a busy time in the garden after short winter days when most growing things have lain dormant. Herb seed should be sown in spring—though seed of some herbs may be sown again in autumn. During springtime many perennial herbs are putting out fresh new growth while others whose tops died away in winter are pushing their way through the soil once again.

Chervil, chives, parsley and tarragon have many uses singly, and when put together they comprise the delicately flavoured and indispensable mixture known as *fines herbes*. The leaves of each are finely chopped in equal quantities and blended together to flavour and garnish omelettes, grilled or baked chicken and fish, salads, soups, mornays, and cooked or uncooked vegetables. The mixture is also delicious as a filling for thinly cut sandwiches to accompany entrées. Sometimes, in recipes, one sees the addition of lemon thyme or other subtly flavoured leaves to *fines herbes*, but this depends on the cook.

For accurate proportions you may either pick the herbs and chop them separately, then measure equal quantities and blend together, or pick the same number of leaves of each herb and chop all together. If using dried herbs, measure equal portions of each, then mix together.

Chervil, parsley and tarragon may be dried for winter use by picking sprays from fully grown plants (be sure to pick these before midday), rinsing in cool water if necessary, then spreading the sprays out on racks in a shady place until they are brittle. The leaves are then stripped off and packed into airtight containers. The usual method of hanging herbs in bunches to dry is not so successful with chervil and parsley, although it can be done with tarragon. Fast drying in a warm oven with frequent turning of the bundles until the herbs are brittle is a good way of preserving the flavour and green colour of chervil and parsley.

Chives are almost impossible to home-dry, but a satisfactory process of freeze-drying chives commercially has been evolved, and these may be bought and added to the chervil, parsley and tarragon for blending as *fines herbes* in winter.

Four pot herbs—borage, dandelion, lovage and sorrel—have been chosen for the section on spring herbs. A pot herb was so called because the leaves, and sometimes the roots too, of certain plants went into nourishing broths and were also used as vegetables, as well as having their place, raw, in salads. They were gathered growing wild along hedgerows, in fields and in woods, and were also cultivated in early gardens, especially in monastery gardens, which are said to be the forerunners of today's kitchen gardens. Many of the large vegetables familiar to us today are descended from these wild herbs.

There were good reasons for eating pot herbs, besides providing something to eat. It was considered necessary to 'cleanse' the blood after a winter diet of the warming, heavy food needed for cold weather. (An old Swiss book advises the taking of a 'spring cure' to cleanse the system, and suggests that one way of doing this is to take your basket to the nearest hedge and cut off a large quantity of sprigs from all the thorny bushes to be found, such as blackthorn, shoots of blackberries, raspberries, pines and gooseberries. These are boiled together in a saucepan of water, sugar is added, and quantities of the tea taken daily for eight days. Pine-needle baths are also advised.)

The cultivation of each pot herb will be dealt with separately because their requirements differ. None of them are usually to be bought commercially dried but there are directions for the home gardener to follow for those pot herbs that can either be dried or preserved in another way.

Certain flowers used in cooking, in perfumed articles, and in hebal remedies bloom in spring too. It is not uncommon to find old recipes for carnation syrup, cowslip wine, marigold pudding, primrose pie, candied violets, rose-petal jam, orange-flower flavoured brandy, pickled broom-flowers, gorse wine, and conserves of rosemary and lavender flowers.

Spring flowers with a surprising number of applications are irises, roses, lavender and violets. Strictly speaking, it is the root of the iris that has the practical uses, but the cheerful blooms carried on long stalks, looking like shining lanterns, give a magic touch to any garden.

Chervil

Chervil (*Anthriscus cerefolium*) is a rewarding herb to grow. It looks like a ferny parsley; the soft, anise-tasting leaves go well in finely textured food, and the aroma complements chives, parsley and tarragon, making a beautifully balanced combination of flavours which go into the *fines herbes* mixture. Another kind of chervil, *Chaerophyllum bulbosum*, has a bulbous root that was eaten extensively in the past, especially during times of plague.

When using chervil in sauces, scrambled eggs or other hot food do not add the chopped leaves until cooking is nearly finished. Chopped chervil leaves can be mixed wtih salad ingredients or used as a garnish for soups and mornays. On the Continent, chervil soup is widely known for its flavour and goodness, and as a special dish to be eaten on Holy Thursday.

Chervil has been traditionally valued as a blood purifier and for its beneficial effect on the kidneys. By eating some of the leaves daily, certain 'hardening' conditions or ailments of the later years will be eased, such as rheumatism or gout. 'Chervil disperses congealed blood in bruises and haemorrhoids, or congestion of the breast of a nursing mother . . . in general it is of real assistance for the "spring cleaning" of the organism', writes Maria Geuter in *Herbs in Nutrition*. For external use, the leaves were made into poultices and applied to swellings and bruises.

It was the Romans who first taught us to use this herb of the Umbelliferae family. Although classed as a biennial, it is best treated as an annual and sown twice a year, in spring and autumn. It flourishes just as lushly in spring as in summer, and will produce a successful crop if the plot is sheltered, with part sun. It is not fussy about soil, but does like water, and if given these conditions will continually self-sow, producing more and more plants all the time. Chervil plants reach a height of 30 cm (12 in) or more and produce small white flowers. It is said that the hot taste of radishes is increased when chervil is grown nearby.

For drying, follow one of the methods given on page 2.

CHERVIL BROTH
(Serves 4 to 6)

I have adapted this broth from a recipe by Vincent la Chapelle, chief cook to the Prince of Orange, 1744. It was a popular soup in the spring 'to sweeten and purify the blood'.

1 veal knuckle
3 leeks, thinly sliced
6 leaves (the tops) of beetroot, finely chopped
salt to taste

3–4 tablespoons finely chopped chervil
2 tablespoons cornstarch
3–4 tablespoons milk

Put the knuckle, leeks, chopped beet leaves and salt into a saucepan, cover with water, and bring to the boil. Simmer with the lid on for 1½ hours. Remove the knuckle and add the chervil. Blend the cornflour and milk together and stir into the broth. If wished, the meat can be taken from the knuckle after cooling, chopped into small pieces, and added to the soup. If a clear, very thin broth is preferred, do not add the blended cornflour and milk.

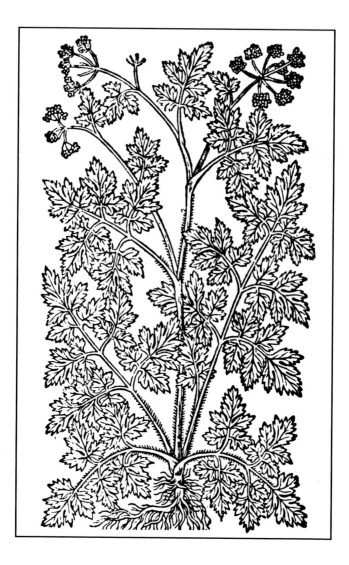

Herbs for all seasons

CHERVIL PASTE

Spread this paste thickly on thin wheat biscuits or on crackers to make a pleasant snack with drinks. Beat 2 eggs with 1 tablespoon milk and salt to taste, scramble in a buttered pan to a creamy consistency, then fold in 1 heaped tablespoon finely chopped chervil. The mixture will be a pale green in colour. Allow to cool before use.

SCALLOPS IN CHERVIL SAUCE

(Serves 6 as an appetiser
serves 4 as a lunch)

Wholegrain parsley sandwiches make an excellent accompaniment
to this delicious dish.

75g (3oz) butter or margarine
500g (1lb) scallops
2 level tablespoons unbleached white flour
315ml (10fl oz) chicken stock
2 tablespoons finely chopped chervil
2 teaspoons grated onion
salt and pepper to taste
125g (4oz) Gruyère cheese, grated
3 tablespoons dried breadcrumbs

Melt 25g (1oz) of the butter in a frying pan and cook the scallops for a few minutes, turning them frequently. (They will exude some moisture making enough liquid with the butter for them to cook in.) Drain the scallops and put them aside. Melt the rest of the butter in a saucepan, blend in the flour, add the chicken stock and stir until the sauce thickens. Fold in the chervil and onion. Season with salt and pepper. Turn the heat off. Add the scallops to the sauce, mix well, then spoon into six individual oven dishes, or into one casserole dish. Top with cheese and breadcrumbs and bake in a moderate oven (175°C, 350°F) for about 5 to 8 minutes until the cheese melts. Serve hot.

Chives

A clump of chives (*Allium schoenoprasum*) in your garden provides one of the most valuable herbs for flavouring. The leaves have a subtle onion taste, which makes them an obvious choice for including in *fines herbes*. Also, they do not have as much sulphur in their composition as onions, and are far more digestible. Chives stimulate the appetite and assist the kidneys.

There are two strains of this species, a variety with very fine grass-like leaves, and another with longer, tubular leaves. A variety known as Siberian chives (*A. schoenoprasum sibericum*) has much larger leaves, which are rather tough. Another kind of chive has a flat leaf with a distinct garlic taste, which is useful when a garlic flavour is wanted without too strong an odour. All belong to the onion family and the genus *Allium*.

For propagating, sow the seeds where the plants are to remain, or in a seed-box, in spring. Autumn planting is possible, but the leaves take much longer to grow. Root division can be carried out in spring or autumn. Chives flourish in moist soil as long as they get some sun and plenty of water: the cold does not hinder them, since they are native to northern Europe and North America. The more you pick them, the better chives will grow. As the mauve tufted flowers appear, nip them off to prevent early dying back of the clump. Chives are at their peak in summer: the green tops wither away when winter comes. Being perennial, they put out new shoots in early spring.

It is almost impossible to harvest and dry chives like other herbs, for they go brown and tasteless, looking rather like old grass cuttings. But the process of freeze-drying them commercially has proved a success: freeze-dried chives are green and already cut up, and have a texture like fine tissue paper, so that they soften immediately when mixed into moist foods. Most dried herbs are stronger in flavour than fresh herbs, but with chives the flavour of the dried herb is not as strong as the fresh. Keep your dried chives in airtight containers away from the light.

As with chervil and parsley, the aroma of chives is destroyed by long cooking, so add the chopped fresh or dried leaves at the last moment. Use them finely chopped as a garnish for soups, mornays, fricassees and salads, and fold them into creamed mash potatoes, cottage or cream cheese, scrambled eggs or cooked rice.

Chives also have their uses in the garden and on the farm: as companion plants for apple-trees chives have prevented apple scab; the leaves may be made into a tea to be used as a spray against mildew on gooseberries and cucumbers, or chopped up and mixed with the mash for young chickens and turkeys.

EGGS IN A GLASS WITH CHIVES
(Serves 1)

A light, simple and nutritious dish—piping-hot eggs cooked in boiling water, shelled and then broken into a small glass goblet and eaten in the usual way with a spoon seem to taste more delicate than eggs eaten from their shells. The whites should be creamy, the yolks soft. We first tasted Eggs in a Glass at the now-vanished Belevedere Hotel, Kings Cross, Sydney.
Bring a saucepan of water to the boil and lower in 2 new-laid eggs. Take the saucepan off the stove, put the lid on, and leave for 10 minutes. Spoon the cooked eggs out of their shells into a nice-looking, warmed, strong glass goblet, and sprinkle with salt, pepper and 1 to 2 teaspoons finely chopped chives. Serve with hot buttered toast.

CHIVES AND SUNFLOWER-SEED CHEESE BALL

(Serves 6)

100g (4 oz) pitted dates, chopped
1 tablespoon orange juice
200g (8 oz) low-fat cottage cheese
50g (2 oz) seedless raisins
2 tablespoons walnut pieces

1 tablespoon finely chopped chives
1 tablespoon finely chopped parsley
salt to taste
50g (2 oz) husked sunflower seeds

Soak the dates in the orange juice for 2 hours or more to soften them. Mash them into the cheese with all the other ingredients except the sunflower seeds. Shape the mixture into a round ball and cover completely with the seeds. Chill. Spread on buttered dark rye biscuits, health bread or pumpernickel (you may prefer to use margarine instead of butter).

Parsley

It is worth growing several kinds of health-giving parsley plants to pick from constantly. Besides curled parsley (*Petroselinum crispum*) there is a fern-leaved parsley (*P. crispum filicinum*), celery-flavoured long-leaved Italian parsley (*P. crispum neapolitanum*), and the turnip-rooted Hamburg parsley, often listed in seed catalogues. The roots of Hamburg parsley are cooked like carrots, parsnips and turnips and eaten as a vegetable, or chopped for soups and casseroles. The sizeable roots of Italian parsley may also be used in the same way.

Originating, it is believed, in Sardinia, parsley has amazing properties that were known in very early times. Homer relates that chariot horses were fed by warriors with the leaves and, being a symbol of great strength, parsley crowned the brave. For its spiritual attributes it was used in temple ceremonies for the dead.

All parts of the herb contain medicinal substances; the root, leaves and seeds are sources of apiol, which is beneficial for the kidneys. The leaves are rich in vitamins A, B and C, and in iron, and assist in the assimilation of food. An essence made from the root has been given for congestion of the kidneys, dropsy and jaundice. A decoction of the bruised seeds was prescribed against plague and intermittent fever, and the oil from the seeds was administered for gynaecological disturbances. Parsley tea made from the leaves is good for rheumatism, kidneys and gall bladder; it assists digestion and encourages circulation.

Because its fresh flavour is unassertive, parsley goes with other herbs in many dishes, and is a complementary ingredient of *fines herbes*. A spray of parsley together with a bay-leaf and a sprig each of thyme and marjoram makes a *bouquet garni* (a bouquet of herbs). The chopped green leaves go into parsley sauce, parsley butter, and parsley jelly; in fact into almost any dish you fancy.

Parsley is a biennial of the Umbelliferae family, and although it often lasts for two years in the garden—especially if the flower stalks are cut off as soon as they appear—it is best treated as an annual, sowing the fresh seeds each year in spring or autumn. Sow the seed either in a seed-box or in the position where the plants are to grow, and remember that they take a little longer than most other herbs to germinate. Parsley does better in rich soil, so if the ground is poor, dig in some fertilizer now and then. For best flavour, grow plants in the sun and give them plenty of water. In very cold climates they need some protection during winter. For drying, see page 2.

In the flower garden, parsley helps roses if grown near by, and in the vegetable garden it is a good neighbour for tomatoes and asparagus.

PARSLEY JELLY

A pleasant accompaniment to chicken or fish dishes.
Wash a big bunch of parsley (about 50 stalks). Place in a saucepan
with enough water to cover, add the peel from a lemon and boil for
about 1 hour. Strain the liquid into a bowl and add the juice of 3
lemons. Measure, allowing a cup of sugar to every cup of liquid. Boil
again until it begins to set. Drop in a little green colouring to improve
the appearance. Pour into jars, seal, and keep in a cool
larder or refrigerator.
This was the recipe as published in my *Penguin Book of Herbs and
Spices*, but recently I added fruit pectin (available from health food
shops) after the sugar was dissolved in the liquid (directions for
quantities are given on the packet).

TABOULEH *see Stray p 10*
5-24-93

*This recipe for a healthy Lebanese salad was given to me
by Maxine de Havilland.*

125g (5 oz) cracked wheat,
known as bulgar
200g (8 oz) finely chopped
parsley
50g (2 oz) finely chopped
spearmint
1–2 tablespoons finely chopped
shallots or white onions

750g (1½ lb) firm, ripe tomatoes,
chopped into little cubes
salt and pepper
185ml (6 fl oz) vegetable oil
the juice of 4 lemons

Soak the cracked wheat in water for 20 minutes to soften, then
squeeze it out. Put the softened wheat into a salad bowl with the
other ingredients in the order given above, then toss well together
and serve.

PARSLEY TEA
(1 cup)

There are two methods of making parsley tea—by infusing the leaves
or by simmering them.
1. Put 1 teaspoon dried parsley leaves (or 2 teaspoons of chopped
fresh leaves) into a small teapot and pour over them 250ml (8 fl oz)
boiling water. Infuse for a minute or two, then strain and drink
'green'. Sweeten if wished.
2. Using the same quantities as above, simmer the leaves in a covered
saucepan for 5 minutes, strain and use.

Herbs for all seasons

Tarragon

French tarragon (*Artemisia dracunculus*) is a perennial from Mediterranean countries. Thriving in a well-drained sunny position in late spring, all summer, and staying verdantly green through autumn, it withers away for a few weeks in winter. As soon as spring comes, the first shoots appear again. Russian tarragon is another variety, with rougher leaves that do not have the tart, anise taste of French tarragon's smooth, pointed leaves. In Continental cookery the use of tarragon is advised 'to temper the coolness of other herbs': the wisdom of this is shown by the delicacy and character it gives to the *fines herbes* quartet.

The name 'tarragon' is adapted from the French *estragon*, which in turn is derived from the Latin *dracunculus*, the diminutive of *draco*, dragon. The herb was known as a cure for venomous bites and stings and also had the reputation of being a 'friend' to the head, heart and liver. Tarragon belongs to a group of aromatic herbs, the artemisias (most of them are bitter as well—for example, wormwood and southernwood). They are all members of the largest plant family in the world, the Compositae, included in which are such different-seeming plants as sunflower, chicory, tansy, lettuce and thistle.

Use this spicy herb in salads, egg dishes, sauces and soups; with fish, poultry, game, liver and kidneys; and to give a unique flavour to vinegar.

In late summer, French tarragon looks as if it is going to flower, but the tight little yellowish buds rarely mature into blossoms, so seed of *Artemisia dracunculus* is virtually unobtainable. (The tarragon seed that is available is nearly always that of Russian tarragon.) The root may be divided or cuttings may be taken in spring or summer. Give the plants a well-drained, warm aspect and water them well in dry weather, otherwise the leaves will wilt badly. One or two plants are usually sufficient for an average household, as tarragon spreads into a bushy shrub 2 to 3 feet tall. If the climate is severely cold, give the roots some protection after the tops die back.

For drying tarragon, cut leafy stalks in summer or autumn in the way suggested on page 2. If preferred, tarragon may be hung in bunches in a warm, airy place to dry.

TARRAGON FISH MOULD
(Serves 5 or 6)

400g (1 lb) fish fillets
800ml (26 fl oz) apple cider
1 bay-leaf
1 spray of thyme
salt to taste
3 packets unflavoured gelatine dissolved in 60ml (2 fl oz) very hot water

4 shallots, finely chopped
1 tablespoon chopped tarragon
300g yoghurt
12 oysters, drained
200g (8oz) prawns, shelled and chopped

Place the fish fillets in an ovenproof dish, pour over the cider, and add the bay-leaf, thyme and salt. Put the lid on and bake in a medium oven (175°C, 350°F) for 30 minutes or until the fillets are cooked. Strain the stock carefully from the pan into a bowl. Bone the fish and flake it finely, then add it with all the other ingredients to the stock, stirring well. Test for flavour, then pour into a rinsed-out mould, place in the refrigerator and leave to set. Turn out on a serving dish and garnish with tarragon sprigs and sliced stuffed olives. Serve with the following sauce.

GREEN CUCUMBER SAUCE

Peel and dice one cucumber, sprinkle with salt and allow to drain.
Wash a small bunch of seedless grapes and pick the grapes from the
stalks. Chop finely a small bunch of parsley. Empty 300g sour cream
into a glass dish, fold in the drained cucumber, the grapes, the
chopped parsley and a pinch of cayenne or a little pepper. Chill.

TARRAGON VINEGAR

Pick leafy stalks of tarragon before the hot sun has drawn out the
aromatic oils, and pack them in a glass jar—or pull the leaves off if
you prefer to, and place these in the jar. Fill the jar up with white or
cider vinegar, screw on the lid, and infuse in a sunny place, if
possible, for two weeks. Strain the vinegar into a bottle and discard
the tarragon. If you have no fresh tarragon, steep 1 heaped tablespoon
of dried tarragon in 625ml (1 pt) vinegar, leaving it for 2 weeks
before using.

Fines Herbes

And now for a few recipes using the *fines herbes* combination of chervil, chives, parsley and tarragon.

BREAKFAST KIDNEYS *FINES HERBES*
(Serves 2)

4 lamb's kidneys
60ml (2 fl oz) water
salt to taste

1 rounded tablespoon cornstarch
1 tablespoon *fines herbes*

Skin the kidneys and remove the fat. Chop the meat fairly small and place it in a saucepan with the water and salt. Simmer until cooked— about 10 minutes. Blend the cornflour with a little extra water and pour this onto the kidneys, stirring until the liquid is thickened. Fold in the *fines herbes* and remove the pan from the stove. Turn the kidneys onto hot buttered toast and serve with grilled bacon.

CHICKEN *FINES HERBES*
(Serves 4)

1–1.5 kg (2½–3lb) chicken
2 tablespoons unbleached flour
1 egg, beaten
2 tablespoons wheat germ

salt and pepper
4 tablespoons vegetable oil
2 tablespoons *fines herbes*

Cut the chicken into portions and thoroughly coat each piece with some of the flour, beaten egg and wheat germ. Dust with salt and pepper. Heat the oil in a shallow flame-proof dish, add the chicken pieces and brown them on top of the stove, turning them to ensure that they are browned all over. Cover with brown paper and place in a medium oven (175°C, 350°F) to bake for 1 hour, turning and basting them once or twice. Remove the paper and continue baking the chicken pieces for another 10 minutes. Lift the portions onto a hot serving dish and sprinkle with *fines herbes*.

STUFFED EGGS MORNAY WITH *FINES HERBES*

(Serves 6 as an appetiser
serves 3 as a lunch)

6 hard-boiled eggs	500ml (16 fl oz) white sauce
salt to taste	200g (8 oz) Gruyère cheese,
freshly ground pepper	grated
1 tablespoon *fines herbes*	

Shell the eggs, cut them into halves lengthways, and scoop the yolks carefully into a bowl. Stir the salt, pepper and herbs into the white sauce, then pour a little of it onto the yolks and mash them to a thick paste. Fill the whites with this mixture. Pour a thin layer of sauce into a buttered ovenproof dish, place the stuffed eggs on this, pour the rest of the sauce over them and cover with a layer of grated Gruyère cheese. Bake in a moderate oven (175°C, 350°F) until the mixture is heated through and the cheese is melted—about 15 to 20 minutes.

FINES HERBES GARLIC BREAD

serves 8 to 10

1 oblong loaf of rye bread	200g (8 oz) butter or margarine,
2 garlic cloves, crushed	softened slightly
2 tablespoons *fines herbes*	

With a sharp knife cut the bread into thinnish slices almost to the bottom crust. Mash the garlic and *fines herbes* into the butter and spread generously on both sides of each bread slice. Wrap the loaf loosely in foil and put in a baking dish in a hot oven (240°C, 450°F) for 10 to 15 minutes, until the bread is crisp. Serve hot.

Fines Herbes

Dandelion

Did you know that the common dandelion (*Taraxacum officinale*) is a traditional health food? In some parts of Europe and America dandelion leaves are still gathered from roadsides and fields to go into spring and summer salads, and as a pot herb into nourishing broths with the addition of other wild greens. This plant is one of nature's gifts, its root, leaves, and flowers all having their special uses. A hidden corner of the garden could perhaps be allowed to harbour a few of these helpful weeds.

It belongs to the Compositae family, and the common name comes from the French *dent de lion*, lion's tooth, referring to the dentate leaf edges, though some think the name is derived from the resemblance of the yellow flower petals to an heraldic lion's golden teeth. The name of the genus comes from the Greek *taraxos*, disorder, and *akos*, remedy, indicating the plant's curative qualities. Arabian writings of the tenth century, Welsh manuscripts of the thirteenth century and English herbals of the sixteenth and seventeenth centuries all mention dandelion as a medicine.

Dandelions self-sow prolifically, and plants are easily recognized by their long, toothed, green leaves and light-sensitive blooms of layered thin petals that eventually turn to downy 'clocks'. Wherever they grow, their bright flower discs glint like newly minted gold coins. For generations children have puffed at the delicate seed-heads to tell the time, the number of puffs to blow them away representing hours. The nectar-filled blossoms are visited by many insects: one observant nature-lover counted ninety-three different kinds of insects, bees being chief among them.

Young dandelion leaves are especially recommended in salads as a blood cleanser, being beneficial to the kidneys and digestion. They are also good for the gall-bladder and liver. For salads, the leaves should be torn to pieces rather than cut, to keep their flavour. The taste is a little bitter, but not unpleasantly so if new small leaves only are picked and then tossed with lettuce leaves in an oil and vinegar dressing. Sometimes blanched cultivated dandelion leaves and roots, which are less bitter, can be bought.

Young dandelion leaves may be cooked alone in a little boiling water, or combined with spinach leaves and cooked in the same way. Before serving, add some grated lemon peel, a knob of butter, and a good pinch of crushed garlic, salt and pepper. A healthful soup is also made with chopped dandelion leaves. The dried leaves are used for teas, and as an ingredient in diet drinks. Dandelion beer and dandelion stout, brewed from the leaves, are favourite country drinks. Dandelion wine, a renowned rustic beverage, is made from the flowers.

Dandelion

Dandelion coffee comes from the roots, which are dried, roasted and ground. It is a natural beverage, without the harmful effects of tea and coffee on the nerves and digestion, does not cause wakefulness, and helps the liver, kidneys and bowels. Some delicious instant dandelion coffees are available in health food shops.

All parts of the plant contain a healthful juice, latex, but the most powerful for medicinal use comes from the root. In the past, dandelion roots were gathered in the fields and the juice was expressed while they were still fresh. Autumn dug roots are considered best.

DANDELION WINE

The flowers must be freshly picked and the petals stripped from them. Put a gallon of these petals into a tub, and pour a gallon of freshly-boiled water over them. Leave, covered, for ten to twelve days, stirring now and then, and then strain the liquid into a preserving-pan and add three to four pounds of sugar according to your taste. Add also the thinly-pared rind of an orange and a lemon and the rest of these two fruits cut into pieces without any trace of white pith or pips. Boil gently together for twenty minutes, and after it has cooled to luke-warm put in a tablespoonful of brewers' yeast or a quarter of an ounce of compressed yeast spread on a piece of toast. Cover again, and leave for a couple of days, then put into a cask, bung it down, and bottle after two months or longer.

AMBROSE HEATH Home-made Wines and Liqueurs

DANDELION TEA

Pour 625ml (1 pt) boiling water onto 25g (1 oz) fresh dandelion leaves. Cover and infuse for 10 minutes. Strain, then sweeten with honey. Drink three times a day.

GREEN DANDELION SALAD
(serves 4 to 6)

8 young dandelion leaves,
washed and dried
½ lettuce, washed and dried
2 teaspoons chopped chives
2 teaspoons whole marjoram
leaves

2 teaspoons whole spearmint
leaves
4 tablespoons vegetable oil
1 tablespoon cider vinegar
1 clove garlic, finely chopped
salt to taste
freshly ground pepper

Tear the dandelion and lettuce leaves into a serving bowl, then add the chives, marjoram and spearmint. Mix the oil and vinegar with the garlic, salt and pepper, pour over the salad and toss well.

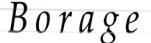

Borage

Borage (*Borago officinalis*) is almost a perennial annual, as it continually self-sows during the year, thriving as well in winter in temperate zones as it does in summer. It was once a valuable pot-herb; the leaves and roots were often used as a vegetable and in nourishing broths.

Old records say that borage originally came from Aleppo, although for many centuries it has been naturalized in most parts of Europe. The plant has a traditional reputation for relieving depression and lifting the spirits, there being many references to this in old manuscripts. Pliny, a Roman soldier and prolific chronicler of the first century, wrote: 'I, Borage, bring always courage'. The seventeenth-century English author and epicure John Evelyn says: 'Sprigs of Borage are of known virtue to revive the hypochondriac and cheer the hard student'. Leaves and flowers are also helpful in combating colds and influenza. A Frenchwoman who has spent nearly all her life in the countryside of her native land tells us that at the onset of a cold, a tisane of borage flowers was taken. Borage is also beneficial to the circulation of the blood, compresses made from the leaves helping to relieve congested veins, especially in the legs when a person has been standing for a long time. The herb is rich in potassium and calcium associated with mineral acids, while the stems and leaves contain saline mucilage: the healing properties of borage are attributed to these saline qualities. It is related to another healing herb, comfrey, and both belong to the Boraginaceae family.

Borage grows 60 to 90cm (2 to 3 ft) high, with a thick central stalk that is hollow. Both the stalk and the branching stems are covered with a hoary stubble of hairs. The broad, fleshy leaves are hairy too although not as prickly, while the clustered buds are covered with a softer down. Seed may be sown in spring, and in temperate climates again in autumn. Once the plant is established it usually looks after itself and will keep coming up, often in unexpected places. If not wanted, the surface-rooted seedlings are easily pulled out. Borage looks its best when allowed to grow in clumps or drifts. The hazy green of the leaves and buds and the massed celestial-blue flowers are an attractive and restful sight in the garden. An occasional pink flower appears among the blue, and there is also a white-blooming kind.

There are many uses for this herb. The whole plant has a faint cucumber flavour, and for this reason the leaves and flowers are traditionally gathered to impart a cooling aroma to wine cups and cider drinks. The chopped leaves of borage make a soup tasty and healthful. Whole young leaves may be dipped in batter, fried, and eaten as a vegetable. When borage leaves are finely minced they make a fragrant addition to salads; and with a dusting of salt and pepper make a delicious sandwich filling. The starry flowers of borage can be crystallized for decorating cakes and trifles, or used fresh as a decoration on sweets and salads. The leaves or flowers of the plant go into the pot for making borage tea. The blossoms also provide an excellent source of honey for bees, and in companion planting it has been noted that borage and strawberries grow well together.

For drying the foliage and flowers of borage, pick unblemished leaves and opened flowers after the dew has gone, and lay them flat on sheets of paper in a shady place. When the leaves are dry and brittle, break them up with your fingers and store in an airtight container. Keep the dried flowers separately, also in an airtight container.

BORAGE LEAF TEA
(1 cup)

Pour 250ml (8 fl oz) boiling water onto 1 teaspoon dried borage leaves (or 1 tablespoon chopped fresh leaves), cover and infuse for several minutes. Strain. Do not add milk, but sweeten with honey if wished.

BORAGE FLOWER TEA
(1 cup)

Bring 250ml (8 fl oz) water to the boil in a saucepan, throw in 1 teaspoon dried flowers (or 2 teaspoons fresh flowers), cover and simmer for 1 minute. Allow to stand for a further 3 minutes. Strain and drink as for leaf tea.

BORAGE SOUP
(Serves 4)

a good handful of borage leaves—about 100g (4 oz)
400g (1 lb) potatoes

940ml (1½ pt) milk
salt to taste
freshly ground pepper

Wash the borage leaves and chop them very finely. Peel and wash the potatoes, cut into small chunks, and cook in boiling water until soft. Drain the potatoes and mash them very smoothly. Gradually add the milk, stirring until well blended. Place the saucepan over low heat, add the chopped borage and the salt, and simmer for 30 minutes. Serve hot or chilled with a spoonful of cream, sour cream or yoghurt, with a borage flower floating in the centre of each bowl.

BORAGE FRITTERS

(Serves 4)

Eat these fritters as a vegetable with roasts and grills or as a tasty accompaniment to fried chicken. The hairiness on the leaves disappears during cooking.

50g (2 oz) unbleached or
wholewheat pastry flour
salt to taste
1 egg

2 teaspoons vegetable oil
2 tablespoons milk
3 small to medium-sized borage
leaves for each person

Mix the flour and salt together in a bowl. Whisk the egg and stir it into the flour, then add the oil and milk and beat until the mixture is smooth. Take the borage leaves one at a time and dip into the batter, coating well, then fry in 2 tablespoons vegetable oil on both sides until golden. Drain on absorbent white or brown paper and serve hot.

Lovage

Lovage (*Levisticum officinale*), originally from the Mediterranean region, is one of the lesser known herbs today, yet it was formerly employed a great deal in medicine and cooking, especially in the fourteenth century when it was grown as a drug plant. Among its components are a volatile oil and resins.

The root, leaves and seeds of lovage were used in herbal medicine for stomach disorders and feverish attacks. An infusion of the root was considered beneficial in many illnesses, including jaundice and urinary troubles. A decoction of the seeds was recommended as a gargle for infections of the mouth and throat, as a drink for pleurisy, and as a lotion for bathing sore eyes. The leaves eaten raw in a salad, or infused dry as a tea, are still recognized as being stimulating for the digestive organs and helpful in remedying gynaecological disturbances. In special diets the chopped leaves may be substituted for hot spices. Lovage was also regarded as an important pot herb.

This herb is a hardy perennial of the Umbelliferae family, and grows from 90 to 150cm (3 to 5 ft) high. In appearance it resembles angelica, although the flavour is different. The flat leaves grow on a branching stem of three and taste rather like both celery and parsley but more strongly of celery; they make an excellent healthful addition to salads, soups, stews, and some sauces. Chop the leaves finely for best results. The hollow stalks and stems are often preserved as a confection in the same way as angelica.

Sow the seed in spring or autumn in a seed-box or where the plants are to stay. Alternatively, the roots may be divided in spring. Grow the plants in well-drained, rich, moist soil in a sunny or semi-shady position. Velvety, greenish yellow flower umbels appear in autumn, and the aromatic seeds that follow are brown when ripe. For drying, unblemished leaves should be cut before the plant flowers, and hung in bunches in a shady place. When ready, crumble the brittle foliage into airtight containers.

LOVAGE SAUCE FOR FISH

Make 315ml (10 fl oz) white sauce (see page 136) and fold in 1 level tablespoon finely chopped lovage leaves.

LOVAGE AND CARROT SALAD
(Serves 4)

1 medium to large carrot,
finely grated
1 large apple,
peeled and grated
2 teaspoons finely chopped
lovage

100g (4 oz) yoghurt
1 tablespoon mayonnaise
salt to taste
lettuce leaves
1 white onion, peeled, then sliced
into rings

Toss the grated carrot and apple with the chopped lovage and the yoghurt, mayonnaise and salt. Arrange the lettuce leaves on a serving plate and mound some of the carrot and lovage mixture onto each leaf. Separate the onion rings and arrange them all over the salad, then decorate with a few whole lovage leaves. Chill.

LOVAGE SOUP
(Serves 3 or 4)

25g (1 oz) butter or margarine
2 tablespoons unbleached flour
625ml (1 pt) chicken stock
150ml (5 fl oz) milk

1 tablespoon chopped lovage
leaves
2 teaspoons lemon juice
salt to taste

Melt the butter in a saucepan, add the flour and blend to a smooth paste. Gradually pour in the stock, stirring until thickened. Add the milk, lovage and lemon juice. Simmer for 15 minutes. Add salt to taste. Put through a sieve or purée in a blender. Serve hot or cold, garnishing each serving with yoghurt or whipped fresh cream, and a sprinkling of finely chopped lovage.

LOVAGE SANDWICHES

Butter thin slices of brown rye or wholewheat bread. Spread half the slices with cream-cheese spread and sprinkle ½ teaspoon finely chopped lovage over each. Top with the remaining buttered slices, cut off the crusts and cut the sandwiches into halves or quarters.

Sorrel

French sorrel (*Rumex scutatus*) grows in clumps like spinach, and has smooth, broad leaves with a refreshing acid taste. It reaches a height of 45 to 60cm (18 to 24 in), and produces tiny round greenish flowers on scarlet-streaked spikes in summer. This species is more acceptable for eating than English or garden sorrel (*R. acetosa*), which has a stronger, sharper flavour. Sorrels, which belong to the Polygonaceae family, are native to Europe and Asia, and have been known as salad and pot herbs for a long time. They are perennials and are closely related to wild dock.

Sorrel is beneficial to the kidneys and aids the digestion. A cooling drink made from the leaves is an old country remedy for fevers, and sorrel is recommended as being good for the blood, especially in spring. It is advisable not to eat the leaves too frequently, as there is some oxalic acid present in the plant, which does not suit everybody.

Sorrel has a reputation for sharpening the appetite, and was highly regarded in the time of Henry VIII. John Evelyn thought much of its addition to salads, saying that it 'imparts a grateful quickness to the rest as supplying the want of oranges and lemons . . .' For a cooling salad, tear up sorrel leaves and lettuce leaves and toss together in a french dressing that has been sweetened slightly with a little honey.

A customary use for sorrel was in a sauce as a accompaniment to omelettes, cold meat and fish, the flavour being of a similar tartness to apple sauce. A piquant, delicious soup made with sorrel is popular in France. It was included in a variety of dishes for its pleasant sharpness, and there is an old recipe dating back to 1682 belonging to Giles Rose, master cook to Charles II, for 'A Tart of the Juice of SORREL'. It has a thin pastry case, and a delectable filling of macaroons, butter, egg yolks, grated green citron, orange flowers, sugar, cinnamon, and the juice of the sorrel expressed by pounding the leaves in a mortar. It is advisable not to cook sorrel in an aluminium saucepan: like spinach, its acid content reacts to the aluminium and it becomes harmful.

Sow seeds in spring or autumn either in a prepared box or where the plants are to remain. Division of roots in spring or autumn is a successful method of propagation too. Grow in light soil in sun or semi-shade, and water in dry weather. Cut off the flower stalks to prevent the plants going to seed.

Sorrel cannot withstand severe winters, but the leaves may be harvested all through the growing period and dried flat in a shady place. Another method, which was published in an old French cookery book of 1796, was to preserve the leaves by cooking them over a slow fire with salt and butter, until all moisture had evaporated; when half cold, the sorrel was pressed into pots. When quite cold, tepid melted butter was poured over the top, and the pots were sealed down and kept in a dry place. Once opened, however, the contents would not keep for more than 3 weeks.

SORREL SAUCE

Wash and chop finely a bunch of young sorrel leaves (about 100g (4 oz)). Melt 25g (1 oz) butter or vegetable margarine in a saucepan (not aluminium) and gently cook the sorrel in it until soft. Blend in 1 rounded tablespoon plain flour and add 315ml (10 fl oz) chicken stock. Stir well until thickened, adding enough salt to flavour. For extra smoothness, 1 tablespoon cream and an egg yolk may be beaten into the sauce immediately it comes off the stove.

SORREL SOUP

(Serves 6)

100g (4 oz) butter or margarine
1 small bunch (100g (4 oz))
sorrel leaves, shredded
2.5l (4 pts) water

400g (1 lb) potatoes, washed,
peeled and diced
salt and pepper to taste
2 egg yolks

Melt the butter in a saucepan (not an aluminium one), stir in the shredded sorrel and simmer until softened. Add the water and the diced potatoes, salt and pepper. Bring to the boil, then simmer with the lid on for 1 hour. Press the soup through a sieve, or purée it in a blender. Reheat in the saucepan. Blend a little of the hot liquid into the beaten egg yolks, pour into the saucepan of soup and stir well, but do not boil again. Chill. Serve with a spoonful of cream in each bowl, and chopped cress or parsley. Serve hot in winter.

SORREL OMELETTE

Blanch a handful of sorrel, fry gently in butter and add some raw parsley and a little cream. While this simmers, make an omelette in the usual way. Thicken the sorrel mixture with an extra egg yolk and pour it at once into the omelette. Fold and serve very hot.

NELL HEATON A Calendar of Country Receipts

Iris

Powdered orris root is an ingredient of pot-pourri, and in the making of pomanders it is always a source of interest. 'Where does it come from?' is a question frequently asked.

Orris powder, or violet powder as it is sometimes called because of its delicate fragrance, is the finely ground root or rhizome of certain flag irises belonging to the Iridaceae family, and may be one of three kinds, *Iris florentina, I. germanica*, or *I. pallida*. The Florentine iris is considered the best for powdered orris. Irises are native to the Mediterranean region, and have been cultivated for their rhizomes in many parts of the world, particularly in southern Europe. They are perennial spring-blooming plants, and besides being of interest in the herb garden their lovely flowers provide splashes of limpid colour, harmonizing with the muted shades of the other herbs. The plant is named Iris after the rainbow goddess.

Orris root is mainly used in perfumery. Ancient Corinth and Macedonia were famous for their unguents made from iris. The arms of Florence were a white iris or lily on a red shield, indicating that the city was famous for these plants. The Florentine iris was often called White Flower de Luce, or Flower de Luce of Florence. It has large white flowers.

I. germanica, or Blue Flower de Luce, is a tall-growing species with large deep-blue flowers. Today there are many hybrids of different colours.

I. pallida has pale-blue blooms.

All these iris flowers exude a faint sweet scent. The roots do not become aromatic until they have been dried for several months.

Iris root has been used in cosmetics and medicines since earliest times. Juice from the rhizomes has a soothing, bleaching effect on the skin, and I have used, and seen others use, an iris jelly hand cream, with remarkable results.

Once the juice, when mixed with wine, was given in the treatment of dropsy. The dried powder was used as a snuff to clear the head, and a pinch of orris powder put into the rinsing water was a favourite method of imparting a fresh fragrance to household linen. Orris powder is used today in the making of pot-pourri and pomanders: it is an essential ingredient because it helps take up any moisture, while also imparting a fragrance.

Iris plants are easy to grow provided they are given a sunny spot in the garden. Their crowns should be exposed and allowed to bake in the sunlight. They do best in well-drained, loamy soil, and need watering in dry weather. They may be propagated by dividing the roots at almost any time, especially in late spring and early summer.

If you are interested in cultivating irises yourself for drying the roots, Mrs M. Grieve in her *Modern Herbal* says that the roots take two to three years to reach maturity. After they are dug, trim off the rootlets, carefully peel the rhizomes, and cut them into pieces. When quite dry, grate and pound the roots to a powder.

A PERFUMED BASKET

This quaint recipe comes from an old book called The Toilet of Flora.

Place a layer of perfumed Cotton extremely thin and even on a piece of Taffety stretched in a frame; strew on it some Violet Powder (Orris) and then some Cypress Powder; cover the whole with another piece of Taffety: nothing more remains to complete the work, but to quilt it, and cut it of the size of the basket, trimming the edges with ribband.

A SCENTED RINSE FOR CLOTHES

Put 1 teaspoon powdered orris root into the final rinsing water in the washing machine, or in a tub.

ORRIS ROOT SACHET FOR DRAWERS AND CUPBOARDS

Mix together 2 tablespoons powdered orris root, a few drops lavender oil and 1 teaspoon ground cinnamon. Fill small muslin bags with the mixture.

Roses

Originally from Persia, the rose has been acknowleged as the queen of flowers for countless centuries. With its beauty and variety of form and colour and its soft perfume it is an enchanting and incomparable flower. Together with the lily, the rose has been a symbol of special qualities since ancient times. Legend says that Zarathustra, the early Persian prophet, taught his followers to breed the nutritious plants we know as fruits and cereals, and it is held by many that fruits are descended from the rose and cereals from the lily.

Roses have long had a religious significance, representing among other things the sufferings of Christ and of the early martyrs. Rose windows, as we know, are a feature of countless cathedrals and churches in the Old and New Worlds.

Writers and poets of many lands have praised the beauty of the rose: one of the earliest poems about this flower was the 'Roman de la Rose' written in France in the thirteenth century and translated in part by Geoffrey Chaucer. Artists, jewellers and sculptors have also helped to make the rose immortal.

There seems no end to the number and variety of dazzling new roses continually being produced, many with long stems and no thorns to speak of, whose flowers hold well and bloom several times a year. But on the whole it is the old roses that have the more lasting appeal. There are disadvantages, to be sure, for their stems are often covered in thorns and they usually flower only every twelve months, in springtime: but during this time their lovely blooms are so abundant and so sweetly scented that no rose-lover worthy of the name can be without one or more specimens in the garden. Some nurseries now list a good selection of the old favourites in their catalogues.

A climber, grown from a cutting taken from a very old garden, has flourished for us in a space of six years, reaching giant proportions over a pergola near the herb garden. In spring the surrounding air seems to shimmer from the cascades of small white roses, each bloom with its fragile, ruffled petals curving over a lime-tinted centre. The vigorous canes make a dense shelter for the many chattering birds that make their nests deep in the bosky sanctuary.

Other old roses that give us great pleasure are silvery-green bushes of pink, white and scarlet moss roses (*Rosa centifolia mucosa*); a cabbage rose (Variegata di Bologna), whose porcelain-pink, tightly frilled petals are amethyst striped; and the Apothecary's Rose (*Rosa gallica officinalis*), also known as the Double French Rose and the Red Rose of Lancaster, which in spring is ablaze for several weeks with plush, crimson semi-double flowers.

The foliage of old roses if softly crinkled and attractive, and there is no need to strip off all the leaves when cutting stems for vases, as the custom is with modern roses.

Roses have many healing and beneficial qualities. It is said that the rose displays the most perfect and harmonious development of plant form. I have taken a fragrant elixir, especially prepared from the juice of fresh rose-petals, as a tonic, and have found an ointment made from rosewater soothing for chapped hands and for the face. A vinegar made from roses is said to be good for headaches caused by the hot sun, compresses being steeped in it and then applied to the forehead.

Roses also go into two French liqueurs, L'Huile de Rose and Parfait Amour. Red and pink rose petals make delicious jams, jellies and syrups, and fragrant rose petals may be used in sandwiches. Scented rose petals were sometimes placed in cherry pies before the crust was put on. Crystallized rose petals are still a favourite confection. Tiny rosebuds or small rose petals can be frozen into ice cubes for punches and cordials. Perfumed roses, newly opened, plucked in the early morning and then dried, go into a pot-pourri mixture or make a fragrant rose pillow to induce sweet sleep.

Buy your roses from a reputable nursery, and make sure you read the guide to their planting and care. Choose a well-drained position for the bushes, preferably a sunny, open place. Although roses like to be fed, it is advisable not to use fertilizers at planting time, but to start when the plants are two or three months old. Compost or cow manure should be used as mulch during the hot summer months. Pruning is carried out in midwinter.

In companion planting it has been found that roses and garlic help each other. Roses have a stronger pefume when garlic is growing nearby. A compost made with garlic and onion refuse is excellent for rose bushes. Parsley, mignonette and lupins as companions to roses in the garden also help to maintain the health of the rose bushes.

A SIMPLE ROSE POT-POURRI

roses
rose-geranium leaves
powdered orris root
best quality rose-geranium oil

ground cinnamon
whole cinnamon stick
whole cloves

The roses
Gather blooms every few days: this is necessary because what may seem to be a large quantity of petals when fresh will be a very small portion when dry. Pick opened flowers after the dew has left them and before the heat of the sun draws out the perfume. Place sheets of paper on the floor of a spare room or in a cupboard. Pull each rose apart gently and spread the petals out to dry on the paper so that they are not touching one another. After a few days, when the petals are crisp, put them into a box and start again with fresh petals. In prolonged wet or humid weather the rose petals will not dry completely, but placing them in a warm oven for a short time will give them the desired crispness.

The rose-geranium leaves
Cut sprays, then snip off the leaves and spread them out to dry. When crisp, store in a separate box.

To mix
When both the petals and leaves are dry, take a glass jar or earthenware crock and place them in it together.

ROSE PETAL TEA SANDWICHES

Butter one end of a loaf of fine-textured wholewheat, rye or white
bread, then with a sharp knife cut the slice as thinly as you can.
Repeat until there are enough slices for sandwiches. Mash some
cream cheese to a spreading consistency with a little top milk and
mix in enough finely chopped, perfumed, red rose petals to colour the
cheese. Spread half the buttered bread with the mixture, close
sandwiches, remove crusts and cut into squares or triangles. Serve
with a scattering of rose petals over the sandwiches for afternoon tea.

ROSE PETAL VINEGAR FOR HEADACHES

Fill a 315ml (½ pt) glass jar with red or pink rose petals. Pour white
vinegar into the jar until full, then cover tightly. Infuse for 2 weeks,
preferably in a sunny position, when the vinegar will be ruby red.
Strain into a bottle that has an airtight top. For headaches pour some
of the scented vinegar into a bowl, soak clean cloths in it, wring out
and apply to the forehead. Repeat until the vinegar
in the bowl is used up.

CRYSTALLIZED ROSE PETALS

Pick one small pink, white or red rose. Pull all the petals off onto a sheet of parchment paper laid on a small oven tray. Stir the white of 1 egg with a fork (do not beat it to a froth), then using a small paint-brush paint both sides of the petals with the egg white. (A quick method is to dip the petals straight into the egg white, coating them well with the fingers.) Shake Superfine sugar over the petals, turn them over and sugar them again. Place the tray in a very slow oven, just turned on with the door open. The petals will harden and candy in about 10–15 minutes, but keep turning them and do not leave for too long or they will go brown. Store in an airtight jar or box between layers of waxed paper. These candied rose-petals make a pretty decoration for a christening cake.

Lavender

Lavender is widely known as a filling for lavender bags and as an ingredient in pot-pourri. It also has soothing properties: a lavender bath at night helps to quieten the peripheral nerves, and a sedative tea to follow which contains dried lavender flowers will work wonders for people suffering from insomnia. A doctor we knew who was interested in natural medicine once said that holding a sprig of lavender under the nostrils and inhaling had the effect of smelling salts, helping to revive and 'draw one together'.

There are a number of different kinds of lavender, the most popular being French lavender (*Lavandula dentata*), English lavender—of which there are several species (*L. vera*, *L. officinalis*, and *L. spica*)—and Italian lavender (*L. stoechas*). All originated in the mountainous regions bordering the western half of the Mediterranean, and belong to the Labiatae family. English lavender was not cultivated in England until about 1568.

French lavender is the hardiest of the species and blooms nearly all the year round. As each flower-flush ends, cut the stalks back to where two more shoots are beginning to branch out: this helps to make a bushy, compact shrub that blooms continuously. Then once a year, at the end of winter, cut the bush back hard to the old wood, leaving just a few leaves. If these measures are carried out regularly the shrub will grow bigger and more thickly than ever in spring and should live for many years. Always grow lavender in well-drained soil, and in full sun if possible. It seems to gain its sustenance from the sun, and will thrive better, with a greater abundance of flowers and a stronger perfume, in poor soil and without fertilizers.

Lavender oil is distilled from the flowers and the sticky serrated leaves of French lavender. Grow lavender from cuttings taken in spring or autumn, or sow seed at these times.

In the case of English lavender, the oil is distilled from the small flowers, which bloom in late spring and into the middle of summer. From silver-grey smooth foliage long spikes shoot up which are thickly covered with highly scented mauve flowers—their perfume is deliciously heady. Before the last flowers on each stalk are fully opened, when their oil content is greatest, pick the stalks and hang them in bunches to dry. At the end of summer, when all have been picked, you may need to cut the bush back hard. It likes the same aspect and growing conditions as French lavender, and is propagated in the same way.

Italian lavender is also highly scented but it is not used for distillation in perfumery as a rule. It is a smaller growing shrub than the others, very bushy, with soft, pointed grey leaves and purple velvety flowers which generously cover the whole plant in winter, spring and on into summer. It is a favourite strewing herb on festive days for churches and houses in Spain and Portugal, and the Arabs use the flowers medicinally. Cultivation and propagation methods are the same as for the other lavenders.

In companion planting, lavenders, in common with other highly aromatic herbs, have a good influence on vegetables growing near by, helping to make healthier plants with more flavour. Lavender also helps to repel moths in clothes cupboards and in carpets. An old anti-moth mixture was a handful each of dried lavender, rosemary, thyme, pennyroyal, and a few cloves mingled together and sewn into muslin bags. A slightly different herb mixture for discouraging moths is given on page 96.

LAVENDER POT-POURRI

200g (8 oz) lavender flowers,
dried and stripped
from their stalks
15g (½ oz) dried thyme leaves
15g (½ oz) dried marjoram
leaves

7g (¼ oz) dried mint leaves
a few drops of best lavender oil
25g (1 oz) powdered orris root
1 teaspoon ground cloves

Mix the lavender flowers and herb leaves together. Stir the lavender oil into the orris powder in a small bowl and mix well, then add it with the ground cloves to the other ingredients. This mixture will hold its perfume for years. It may go into sachets or into bowls.

LAVENDER BATH

Pick a bunch of lavender with its leaves, and tie in a piece of cheesecloth to make a bag. Place in a hot bath while the water is running and leave there during the bath.

CONSERVE OF LAVENDER FLOWERS (AS ICING)

This is a variation of the conserve of lavender flowers in The Queen's Closet Opened, *by W. M., cook to Queen Henrietta Maria, 1655. It has a delicious, fragrant taste and looks attractive.*

10 stalks English or French
lavender flowers

4 tablespoons confectioner's
sugar
4 teaspoons rosewater

Rub the flowers off the stalks and chop finely, making about 1 tablespoon of chopped petals. Beat the sifted confectioner's sugar and flowers together in a bowl, then add enough rosewater to make a thin paste. Spread sparingly on top of plain sweet biscuits or over a plain cake, and allow to set.

A charming idea adapted from that useful little book *Lotions and Potions*. Pick English lavender in full flower but before it begins to drop. Take about 20 heads (an even number is desirable) on stalks as long as possible. With mauve ribbon 65 to 125mm (¼ in to ½ in) wide, tie the heads tightly together just below the flower spike, leaving one end of the ribbon about 23cm (9 in) long and the other end as long as possible. Bend the stems carefully over just below the ribbon knot, spacing evenly over flower spikes. Interweave the long end of ribbon through alternate stalks, going round and round the stems until the flowers are enclosed. At this point, twist the ribbon several times round the stalks to secure them, and tie in a bow, with the short end (which must be brought down with the flower heads) underneath the weaving.

Violets

Did you know that violet leaves have a delicate and pleasing taste and make a delightful addition to a mixed green salad? Both the leaves and flowers of this humble small plant (*Viola odorata*) are helpful to the kidneys, as well as having other healing attributes, while the rhizomes or roots have similar emetic properties to ipecacuanha.

Violet flowers are slightly laxative, especially when made into syrup of violets: in olden times writers advocated syrup of violets as a remedy for sleeplessness, pleurisy and quinsy; and it has been found that certain elements in the flowers possess undeniable qualities as ingredients of an expectorant. Violet milk, made by steeping the flowers in milk, is said to be good for the complexion. A wine made from sweet violet flowers was popular with the early Romans, and violet vinegar, made by steeping the flowers in white vinegar, has a delicious scent and a beautiful colour. Violet tea, honey of violets, violet tablets, conserve of violets, crystallized violets, violet marmalade and violet cakes are other delectable recipes of bygone days. Crystallized or sugared violets are easy to prepare, and add an enchanting touch to spring desserts and little cakes. Mauve and purple blooms are frequently seen, but there are also red, pink and white varieties with both single and double flowers.

Preparations of fresh violet leaves were once used internally and externally as a treatment for certain malignancies, especially in the throat and mouth. Violet-leaf infusions, violet-leaf fritters and violet leaves in herb pottages were also once in common usage.

Violets are perennial, and belong to the Violacea family, in which there are many species. They are native to Europe, northern Asia and North America.

Violets are propagated either by taking rooted runners in early winter or by sowing seed in autumn. Choose well-dug sandy loam for the plants in an open position, and allow 12 inches between each row. With the coming of summer apply a mulch of leaf-mould or well-decayed cow manure, and water well in dry weather. It is also advisable to grow violet plants in as clear an atmosphere as possible. Flowers appear in winter and spring and may be dried for teas by picking them before noon, then spreading them out on racks, or on sheets of paper, in a shady place. When ready, pack into airtight containers.

VIOLET ICE CREAM
(Serves 6 to 8)

1 large bunch fresh violets
315ml (10 fl oz) milk
6 egg yolks
75g (3 oz) sugar

315ml (10 fl oz) cream
violet food colouring
12 crystallised violets

Wash the violets and put them in a saucepan with the milk. Scald gently over low heat, then cover the pan and stand it aside for 10 minutes. Strain the milk and discard the violets. Whisk the egg yolks and sugar together, add to the strained milk, and stir over low heat until thick, removing from the stove while still stirring. (If it curdles, whip well with a rotary beater.) Beat the cream until thickened, then fold into the custard. Add a few drops of food colouring to make a soft mauve, then pour into a chilled refrigerator tray and place in the freezing compartment. Stir once or twice during freezing. Embellish the ice cream with crystallized violets before serving.

CRYSTALLIZED VIOLETS

Prepare in the same way as crystallized rose-petals (see page 40).

VIOLET FLOWER TEA

For a soothing beverage for cold or bronchitis sufferers, pour 315ml (10 fl oz) boiling water onto 1 teaspoon dried violets. Cover and leave to infuse for 5 minutes. Strain, then sweeten with honey.

VIOLET MILK FOR THE COMPLEXION

Pour 315ml (10 fl oz) warm milk over a large handful of violet flowers. Steep for several hours, strain, and keep the milk in a stoppered bottle in the refrigerator. Soak cotton-wool balls in this violet milk and pat all over the face and neck twice a day.

VIOLET LEAF SALAD

As violets are evergreen plants, this salad can be made nearly all the year round. For two people, pick 6 to 8 young violet leaves, wash them and pat dry. Tear up a few lettuce leaves, and mix the greens together in a salad bowl. Sprinkle with salt and pepper. Just before serving, toss the salad in 1 tablespoon vegetable oil mixed with 1 teaspoon lemon juice. If the violets are in flower, toss a few flowers into the bowl.

AN INFUSION OF VIOLET LEAVES

Take 60g (2 oz) freshly picked violet leaves, wash them and place in a stone jar. Pour over them 625ml (1 pt) boiling water. Close up the jar and allow it to stand for 12 hours in a cool place. Strain the liquid into a stoppered bottle and keep it cool to prevent it from turning sour. Drink the tea cold two or three times a day, a small teacupful at a time. The tea should be made fresh every day, and any left over should be thrown away.

SYRUP OF VIOLETS

This is an old recipe from Mrs M. Grieve's *Modern Herbal.*

To 1 lb of sweet violet flowers freshly picked, add 2½ pints of boiling water, infuse these for 24 hours in a glazed china vessel, then pour off the liquid and strain it gently through muslin; afterwards add double its weight of the finest loaf sugar and make it into a syrup, but without letting it boil.

Another old recipe says to let the syrup boil only once or twice at the most. To prevent its boiling continuously, stand the vessel holding the syrup in a fairly deep pan of boiling water while cooking.

Summer

PLENTEOUS SALAD HERBS
*bas.il bergamont cress mustard
nasturtium salad burnet
mint and balm*

SOME OLD-FASHIONED TREES
bay elder lemon verbena

When skies are blue and days are bright
A kitchen-garden's my delight,
Set round with rows of decent box
And blowsy girls of hollyhocks.

Lavender, sweet-briar, orris. Here
Shall Beauty make her pomander,
Her sweet-balls for to lay in clothes
That wrap her as the leaves the rose.

KATHARINE TYNAN   The Choice

Fresh salads with a plentiful addition of tasty herbs have an appealing relish in hot weather, helping to stimulate flagging appetites and being otherwise good for the health.

Basil, bergamot, cress, mustard, mint, balm, nasturtium and salad burnet are all excellent salad herbs besides having other uses, and they all grow through summer and on into autumn or later. With so many different herbs to choose from, salads need never be monotonous. Frost-tender basil should be dried in autumn for winter use, along with some of the perennial herbs—bergamot and the mints, for instance—that wither back to ground level during the coldest months. Salad burnet has flourishing evergreen leaves for picking all the year long.

It is in summer that the magic of early morning draws one into the garden soon after dawn, where, surrounded by the peaceful clamour of Nature, another dimension is experienced. Working among the plants, turning the soil, unhurriedly inhaling the various scents of flowers, foliage and earth, wondering at the purity of dew crystals while birds, insects and lizards watch in friendly curiosity, makes you think that the 'little people' are not far away:

In old dayes of the King Artour
Of which that Bretons speken gret honour,
All was this land fulfilled of faerie:
The elf-quene with hire jolie company
Daunsed full of te in many a grene mede;
This was the old opinion as I rede.
I speke of many hundred yeres agoe,
But now can no man see non elves mo.

CHAUCER

In the same mood it is even possible to gather the dew if patient enough. Sir Hugh Plat's *Delights for Ladies* (1609) tells us how to 'gather and clarify maydew':

When there hath fallen no rain the night before, then with a clean
and large sponge, the next morning, you may gather the dew
from sweet herbs, grass or corn. Strain your dew and expose it
to the sun in glasses covered with papers or parchment, pricked
full of holes. Strain it often, leaving it in the sun in a hot place till
it grows white and clear, which will take the best part of the summer.
Some recommend Maydew gathered from Fennell and
Celandine to be most excellent for sore eyes, and some recommend
the same (prepared as before) above Rosewater for
preserving of fruits and flowers.

If you do not have a garden or a window box, a number of herbs mentioned here are available in their dried form in health food shops or grocery stores. Some of the salad herbs which are not usually dried are found growing wild by roadsides, in fields and on disused plots of ground, and are sometimes sold in greengrocers' shops.

There are several trees which are an asset to the herb garden. Two of these, the bay and lemon verbena, have powerfully scented leaves, while the flowers and berries of the elder-tree are valuable in different ways. Each has its uses in herbal recipes for cooking, medicine, perfumed articles or beauty care. None of them have been easy to find in nurseries, but recently, with a revival of interest in herbs and old-fashioned shrubs and trees, they are finding their way back into garden catalogues.

Bays and lemon verbenas are quite well known, and elder-trees are often seen in gardens, but did you know that elderflowers and elderberries have as many diverse uses as most herbs? I have included a number of uses for the blossoms and fruit of this tree in particular, as well as some interesting recipes for the others.

Basil

Spicy basil is one of the most popular of all aromatic herbs. It belongs to the Labiatae family, whose plants are renowned for their pungency. Two excellent kinds are sweet basil (*Ocimum basilicum*) which grows 70 to 90cm (2½ to 3 ft) high and has fairly large fragrant leaves, and bush basil (*O. minimum*), a small shrubby plant growing no higher than 15 to 30cm (6 to 12 in) with a thick mass of tiny scented leaves. Both are annuals, and their flavour is almost identical.

Basil is revered in India, its native home, where as tulasi it is a sacred herb: basil plants are cherished also because of the belief that they disinfect and enliven germ-laden air. The herb spread from India centuries ago to become part of the folklore of other countries, and was well known to the ancient Greeks and Romans.

Besides being useful for flavouring, basil also helps to counteract the effects of unwholesome food, and like so many other herbs, is an aid to digestion. An infusion of the green leaves in boiling water is said to be a remedy for nausea and vomiting. Dried basil leaves in the form of snuff have been used as a cure for nervous headaches and to relieve head-colds, and the seeds were once laid upon venomous bites and taken internally as an antidote to poison.

Sow basil seed in late spring—after all cold-weather snaps have gone, otherwise the young seedlings will blacken and die. Basil likes plenty of sun, porous soil, and needs water during dry weather. It does not grow well near rue, one of the bitterest of herbs. Encourage branching by nipping the centres of the young plants, and watch for snails and slugs. To capture all the flavour for drying, harvest the branches after the dew has evaporated and before the plant flowers. Tie the leafy stalks in bunches and hang in a shady, airy place until dry, then rub off the leaves and crumble them into stoppered or screw-topped containers.

Basil goes well with different kinds of food: it is a celebrated herb for use with tomatoes and in pasta dishes, and it also goes especially well with eggplant, squash and zucchini, with fish and shellfish, and in salads and chicken casseroles. Pick a big bunch from the garden and place it in a jug of water in the kitchen to have it handy and to make the most of this summer herb all through the warm weather.

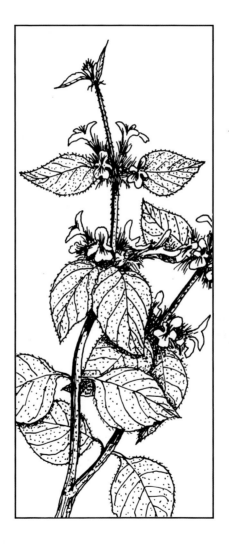

BASIL SAVOURIES

These may be prepared an hour or two in advance and kept in the refrigerator. Butter thin slices of rye bread and cut them into bite-size pieces, leaving the crusts on. Cover thickly with cheese spread, and lightly press a small whole basil leaf into the centre of each piece.

TUNA BASIL MOULD
(Serves 6)

We often have this dish for lunch in hot weather because it tastes cool and light and is low in calories. A nice complement to it is a crisp cold salad made with torn-up lettuce leaves, sliced cucumber, olives, seedless grapes and various herb leaves, all tossed together in an oil and vinegar dressing.

1 x 375g (15 oz) can tuna	1 teaspoon ground ginger
1 x 385g (15½ oz) can tomato purée	60ml (2 fl oz) hot water
2 tablespoons finely chopped basil	3 packets unflavoured gelatine
1 tablespoon finely chopped onion	200g (8 oz) plain yoghurt
	salt and pepper

Empty the tuna onto a plate with its liquid, discard the bones and any skin, and break up the fish with a fork. Put the tomato purée, basil, onion and ginger into a saucepan and heat gently without boiling. Meanwhile, pour the hot water onto the gelatine and blend until clear, then stir it into the warmed tomato mixture, turning the heat off at the same time. Fold in the yoghurt and tuna, and add salt and pepper to taste. Pour the mixture into a wetted mould and set in the refrigerator. Serve unmoulded on a flat dish surrounded by a wreath of green basil sprigs, cress leaves or fennel fronds.

FOUR-HERBS VINEGAR

Cut basil, borage, mint and chives just before the plants flower. Bruise the leaves and pack them into a glass jar. Heat white vinegar and pour over the leaves. Cover and infuse for 14 days, shaking occasionally. Strain, then store in glass bottles with screw-top lids.

BAKED EGGS IN TOMATOES WITH BASIL
(Serves 4)

This is a pleasant dish for a light lunch.

4 large, ripe, firm tomatoes
4 tablespoons soft
breadcrumbs
1 heaped tablespoon
chopped basil

1 tablespoon chopped chives
salt and pepper
4 eggs
4 pieces hot buttered wholegrain
toast, crusts removed

Cut the tops off the tomatoes. Scoop the centres out carefully with a teaspoon into a bowl, and mash with a fork. Add the breadcrumbs, basil, chives, salt and pepper to the tomato pulp and mix to a thick paste, adding more breadcrumbs if necessary. Break an egg into each tomato, then heap some of the breadcrumb mixture on top. Place in an ovenproof dish and bake in a moderate oven (175°C, 350°F) until the tomatoes are soft but still able to hold their shape (this takes 30 to 40 minutes). When ready, place the baked stuffed tomatoes on toast and garnish them with sprigs of basil.

Bergamot

Bergamot (*Monarda didyma*) with its fragrant leaves and soft, honeyed petals, is a very refreshing herb to use in hot weather. This perennial is a member of the Labiatae family and closely akin to the mints. A native of America, it is often called Oswego Tea, an infusion of the leaves having been widely used by the Oswego Indians.

The early American settlers discovered bergamot as a tea, and in nineteenth-century England it was even preferred for a time to China tea. As well as being an aromatic, invigorating beverage, the tea is regarded highly as a remedy for sore throats, colds and chest complaints. One of the main essences of the plant is thymol. Another attractive name for bergamot is bee balm, so-called because bees continually visit the blossoms.

The plants are propagated by sowing seed in spring, or by root division in spring or autumn. There are several different types of this herb and the colours range from pink, mauve and magenta to rich red. It is the red bergamot, Cambridge Scarlet, that is grown most frequently.

Bergamot will not flourish unless established in the right position: the creeping roots like to be kept cool and moist, and the plant furthermore, likes sunlight, morning sun being preferable. In dry weather it is a good idea to keep the roots well covered with a mulch of grass clippings, and water them well from time to time. It starts to grow rapidly as soon as spring comes, the stems reaching 90 to 120cm (3 to 4 ft) in height, and the spidery pom-pom flowers begin to appear in early summer. When flowering has ceased, cut all stalks back to the ground.

For drying, pick long stalks before the plant blooms, and dry in the same way as basil (see page 54).

BERGAMOT TEA
(Serves 1)

If using fresh leaves allow 3 teaspoons, coarsely chopped, to a cup.
Pour boiling water over the leaves in a crockery teapot, cover and
allow to stand for 3 minutes. Strain, do not add milk, but sweeten
with honey if wished. For dried leaves allow 1 teaspoon to a cup and
make in the same way.

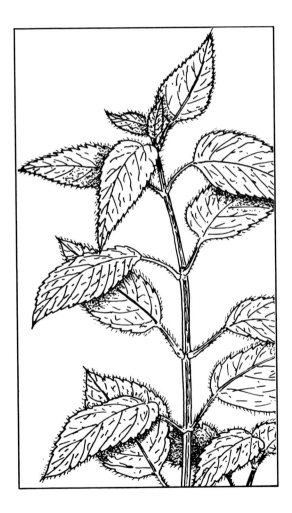

Bergamot flowers are edible, and there is nothing prettier than this unusual flower salad combining red bergamot petals, blue borage flowers, yellow nasturtium flowers and tiny pink rose-petals, with the different colours sparkling like confetti among the green lettuce leaves. Wash and dry lettuce leaves and tear them into a wooden or glass bowl. Add several small whole bergamot leaves. Gather 2 or 3 bergamot flowers, 8 to 12 borage flowers, 3 nasturtium flowers and a small pink rose. Wash the flowers only if necessary, for some of the fragrance may disappear. Toss the lettuce in an oil and vinegar dressing (3 tablespoons oil to 1 tablespoon vinegar or lemon juice). Pluck off the bergamot petals into the bowl, throw in the borage flowers whole, pull the nasturtium petals apart and add them, then add the carefully torn-off rose petals. Give the salad another gentle toss before serving.

Cress and mustard

Cress is easy to grow, and may be used throughout the year for flavouring and garnishing. During the hot months its welcome biting taste spikes salads; cress sandwiches are delicious on a warm summer's day, and chilled cress soup is refreshing. Cress in soup is not new, for it was once a pot herb.

There are a number of types of cress, all rich in iron. They belong to the Cruciferae family, which has no poisonous plants among its two thousand species. Watercress (*Nasturtium officinale*) is found growing wild in running streams, and may be cultivated by home gardeners in containers. There are also varieties of land cress (*Lepidium sativum*), originally from Persia, with the same flavour. Little baskets or bunches of cress are readily available in shops in some parts of the world, but when it is difficult to find these, and if bunches of fresh watercress in greengrocers' shops are unobtainable, we can recommend three types of land cress which grow well in the garden: they are popularly known as curled cress, French cress, and American upland cress.

Watercress is a hardy perennial, coming originally from Europe and parts of Asia. It has small round leaves of dark green, and tiny white flowers, and like other cresses its taste resembles that of nasturtium. (The true nasturtium with its creeping habit and show of flowers is sometimes known as Indian cress.) If you have a shallow trough where the water can be changed, make a loamy bed of soil for watercress seedlings (which have been started from seed in a box) and place under a tap in the shade. As the seedlings grow, gradually fill the trough with water, carefully tipping the

water away once or twice a week and then refilling. Constant cutting leads to repeated branching of the plants and, in summer, clipping even closer will help to prevent flowering.

Curled cress is similar in appearance to curled parsley, only the leaves are fleshier and the flavour is hot and sharp. Treat curled cress as an annual. We sow it straight into the ground in a semi-shady place in spring and again in autumn. Apart from watering the plants in dry weather, there is no need to give them special attention. If the soil is poor, it may be enriched with fertilizer.

Treat American upland cress as an annual too, and sow in spring and autumn. The plant grows in a full rosette of dark-green jagged leaves up to 15cm (6 in) long, with a typically hot flavour. Growing conditions are the same as for curled cress.

French cress has pale-green leaves, quite undivided but with a frilled edge, and resembles young lettuce when growing. Although it bears no likeness to the other cresses, once again the flavour of the leaves is pepper-hot. It is an annual, so cultivation is the same as with curled cress or American upland cress.

Herbs for all seasons

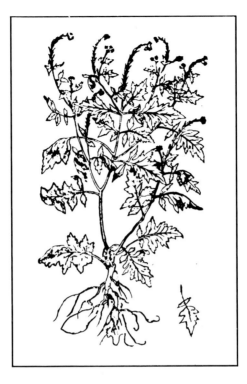

Mustard (*Brassica alba*) is also a member of the Cruciferae family, and is often sown with cress to go with it in salads and sandwiches. Mustard is an annual, and was once a familiar pot herb. Because of quick germination it has been used by exhibitors at country shows to grow in various shapes, which may depict an animal, such as a cow, amidst collections of vegetables. For this, the mustard is usually sown onto moist fibrous loam within the shape, and in warm weather it should be ready to exhibit in six to eight days. If combining mustard with cress for this, sow cress three days earlier, since it takes longer for cress to develop a similar state of growth. Growing conditions in the garden for mustard are identical to those for cress.

Mustard leaves have a strong, hot flavour, and mustard greens are an old favourite as an ingredient of soups to help clear the blood. Wild herb soup is made from a mixture of the young leaves of certain herbs, either growing in the garden or found wild in the fields—they may be dandelions, docks, violet leaves, watercress, and nettle tops. These are washed and put in a saucepan with water, a meaty ham bone, and a few cloves of garlic. Simmer covered for 1 hour but during the last half-hour add 2 or 3 potatoes, peeled and cut into dice, and some salt to taste. Serve the leafy soup hot with some of the potatoes in each bowl, and some of the ham from the bone, chopped up. If you wish, omit the ham bone and add sliced hard-boiled eggs with the potato to each serving.

Mustard seed used in cooking and in the making of culinary mustards comes from the ripe seed of this herb. Those famous old remedies for head colds and inflammation of the chest, mustard plasters and mustard foot-baths, are also made from powdered mustard seed. The herb is native to Europe, Asia and North America.

A similar herb to both cress and mustard, and another member of the Cruciferae family, is rocket (*Hesperis matronalis*), also known as vesper-flower, dame's violet and roquette. It is native to Italy and grows wild in many parts of Europe and Asia. The leaves have a pronounced mustard flavour and are excellent in salads and sandwiches. The flowers give out a sweet perfume in the evening, and are white with lavender markings. It is a biennial, but in warm climates it tends to go to seed and disappear rather quickly, especially in summer. Try sowing seed in spring, and again in autumn, if you have this problem. The best flavour of the leaves, which were once eaten to prevent scurvy, is captured if they are gathered before the plant starts to flower. For medicinal purposes it is advisable to pick when in flower. In former days a strong dose of the prepared leaves was given in place of ipecacuanha to induce vomiting.

CRESS SANDWICHES

Spread thin slices of pumpernickel or wholewheat bread with butter or margarine. Chop cress leaves of any type and heap them on the bottom half of each sandwich. Cover with the top slice, cut off the crusts, and cut the sandwiches into squares or triangles. A thin film of Marmite can go on the bread before the cress is put on. These fresh-tasting sandwiches go well with soup or an entrée.
Chopped cress on buttered plain biscuits is also tasty. Young mustard leaves may be chopped and mingled with the cress.

CRESS AND MUSTARD SALAD
(Serves 4)

100g (4 oz) cress leaves
100g (4 oz) young
mustard leaves
½ lettuce
1 ripe pear or eating apple
juice of ½ lemon

salt
3 tablespoons vegetable oil
2 to 4 teaspoons apple cider
vinegar
1 clove of garlic, crushed

Wash and dry the cress, mustard and lettuce leaves. Tear all leaves into a salad bowl. Peel and core the pear or apple, chop into small dice, toss in the lemon juice, then add to the salad with a sprinkling of salt. Combine the oil, vinegar and garlic, pour over the greens and toss well, then serve.

CHILLED CRESS SOUP

400g (1 lb) potatoes, washed,
peeled and diced
1 white onion, chopped
625ml (1 pt) water

625ml (1 pt) milk
100g (4 oz) finely chopped
cress leaves
salt to taste

Put the potatoes and onion into a saucepan with the water and simmer with a lid on for 1 hour. Press the mixture through a sieve, or purée it in a blender, then return it to the saucepan on low heat. Heat the milk in a separate saucepan and stir into the purée until thoroughly blended. Add the cress and salt, and take off the stove. Chill the soup well, then pour it into cold bowls with a teaspoonful of yoghurt or sour cream, and a cress leaf, on each serving. For a light lunch add baby prawns, or a fine julienne (thin strips) of chicken, to the soup.

Nasturtium

An ancient oriental custom which has come down to us is eating the petals of nasturtium. The leaves and flowers of nasturtiums are often added to salads and sandwiches, and the flower-buds and fruits are often pickled in vinegar and used in the same way as capers.

Nasturtium (*Tropaeolum majus*) belongs to the Cruciferae family. The leaves are round and flat, with spider-web veins of milky-green. Their keen, hot taste makes them a useful replacement for pepper in many dishes; and because of the similarity of its flavour to the biting flavour of cress, nasturtium is sometimes called Indian cress. As the leaves have a high content of vitamin C, their use helps to relieve symptoms of colds and influenza.

Pick young tender leaves and eat them whole in salads or use as sandwich fillings; chop them finely for sauces, cheese dips and cheese spreads.

The pollen-filled luminous blooms of nasturtium have frilled, silken petals in intense colours varying from bright yellow and vermilion to deep orange; they taste like the leaves, but are not as strong. Flowers for salads and sandwiches may be eaten whole or gently torn apart. As a garnish the flowers should be left whole.

This hardy annual will grow almost anywhere, but well-drained soil in a sunny place will ensure more flowers. Sow seed in spring where the plants are to grow, and keep the ground moist until the seedlings are established. Propagation can also be by runners with hair roots or by division of the main root system in spring, summer and autumn.

Flowering begins in summer and continues into the cool weather. The plant has a climbing or creeping habit and will spread over large areas. There are compact forms for border edging.

Nasturtiums in the garden are useful pest-controllers, helping to keep away many destructive insects, especially when planted under trees that suffer from woolly aphis. It is said that they also aid nearby radishes and potatoes.

For harvesting the leaves to dry, pick them before the plant flowers, and spread them flat in a shady place until ready to pack, whole or crumbled, into airtight containers.

NASTURTIUM SALAD

Take a small, washed and crisped lettuce and tear the leaves into a
salad bowl, add 6 finely cut-up nasturtium leaves. Toss the salad in 2
tablespoons of vegetable oil and 2 teaspoons of white vinegar.
Arrange a few whole nasturtium flowers on top of the
salad and serve.

CHILLED PEANUT AND NASTURTIUM SOUP
(Serves 4)

775ml (10 fl oz) hot water
4 teaspoons Marmite
100g (4 oz) roasted peanuts
3 or 4 nasturtium leaves,
chopped roughly

salt to taste
315ml (25 fl oz) milk
nasturtium flowers

Pour the hot water onto the Marmite and stir until dissolved, making a broth. Place the peanuts, 250ml (8 fl oz) of the broth, the nasturtium leaves and the salt together in a blender and purée until smooth. Empty the peanut mixture into a saucepan, stir in the rest of the broth and milk, simmer for 10 minutes, then chill. Float a nasturtium flower—or one petal if you prefer it—on each serving.

Salad Burnet

Salad burnet (*Sanguisorba minor*) is not a well-known herb, probably because the leaves have no aroma when dried, yet the newly picked foliage has a dewy, fresh flavour with a number of special uses.

The botanical name for salad burnet is also sometimes listed as *Poterium sanguisorba*. Frequently, several of the leaves of this plant were added to wine cups and other beverages, the herb having the same power as borage to 'cheer the heart, and drive away melancholy . . .' Its properties are also tonic. *Poterium* is from the Greek *poterion*, drinking cup. The rest of the name was formerly its old generic name, and comes from *sanguis*, blood, and *sorbere*, to staunch, because of the herb's former reputation of being able to stop bleeding, for which both the leaves and the root were recommended. It belongs to the Rosaceae family.

There is another burnet too, not to be confused with this one, called *Pimpinella saxifraga*, which is of the same family as parsley and dill but is not used in cooking.

Salad burnet grows 30 to 45cm (12 to 18 in) high and is an attractive herb for borders. The small round leaves look as if they have been cut out with pinking scissors and then fastened in eight or nine neat pairs along each side of a slender stalk, making one long leaf or spray. In form the whole plant is a froth of sprays which fall gracefully from the centre outwards. In summer many straight stalks shoot quickly upwards bearing unusual raspberry-like flower-heads.

Apart from needing water in dry weather, burnet is so hardy it will grow in all types of soil and under any conditions, even through cold winters. It is a perennial, and self-sows readily; flower stalks may be cut off when they appear, to prevent too rapid seeding. Seeds are sown in spring and autumn, or roots may be divided at this time.

Add sprays of salad burnet to tossed green salads, or use them to garnish chilled moulds and aspics. For sandwiches, lay whole leaves pulled from their stalks on buttered brown bread (add a whisper of Marmite first if you like). The leaves may be chopped but there is no need, since they are soft. Leafy stalks of salad burnet also go into wine cups, punches and fruit cordials.

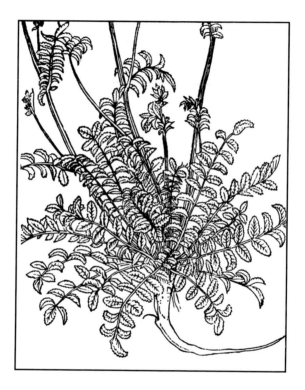

WHITE WINE CUP WITH SALAD BURNET

2 bottles dry white wine	400ml (13 fl oz) soda water
1 wineglass brandy	a bunch of salad burnet sprays
1 wineglass blackcurrant juice	12 strawberries

Mix all ingredients together in a large serving bowl. Chill. Add ice cubes before serving.

HONEYDEW MELON WITH SALAD BURNET AND HAM

(Serves 6)

A cool first course for a hot weather meal. If honeydew melon is not available, other suitable fresh fruits may be used instead, such as casaba, canteloup or ripe pears.

6 lettuce leaves, washed and dried

1 honeydew melon cut into 6 segments and peeled

6 thin slices ham (preferably smoked), fat and rind removed

a few sprays of salad burnet

Arrange the lettuce leaves and the melon segments on 6 small plates with the ham slices. Pull the burnet leaves from the central stem and scatter about a dozen over each melon slice. Serve chilled, with French dressing and freshly ground pepper.

Salad Burnet

SALAD BURNET AND BEETROOT JELLY
(Serves 4)

Beetroot jelly is an old summer favourite. This recipe is rather different from any other—not only is it flavoured with cool salad burnet but it is set with powdered agar, a seaweed product often used in place of gelatine by vegetarians. This is not its only advantage: agar jelly sets quickly without refrigeration, and remains jellied on the hottest day without being kept cold. If you decide to try powdered agar instead of gelatine for setting, here are a few tips: it must first be boiled in the liquid intended for jellying, 1 teaspoon of agar powder to 625ml (1 pt) liquid, boiling time 2 to 3 minutes. Add the acid ingredients, such as vinegar or lemon juice, when boiling is completed and while the liquid is still hot. One summer's day with the temperature at 35°C, (80°F), this jelly set firmly in a jelly-mould on my kitchen table in ten minutes, and was glossy hard within half an hour.

1 bunch beetroot	1 teaspoon caraway seed
salt to taste	or dill seed
1 teaspoon powdered agar	1 tablespoon apple cider vinegar
1 tablespoon clear honey	
1 tablespoon chopped salad burnet	

Cut the tops off the beetroot, wash the beets well and place in a saucepan with water to cover. Add the salt, simmer until tender. Peel the beets and cut them up. Arrange in a dish. Measure 625ml (1 pt) of the liquid, return it to the saucepan and test for salt, adding a little more if necessary. Mix the agar to a runny paste with a little water and stir it into the juice in the saucepan together with the honey, salad burnet and caraway seed. Simmer for 3 minutes. Take the pan off the stove and stir in the vinegar.

Pour the hot liquid over the beetroot and leave to set. The dish may be decorated with whipped low-fat sour cream and a sprinkling of whole burnet leaves stripped from their stalks.

Mint and Balm

Versatile mint with its invigorating qualities is a welcome addition to all kinds of salads and cooling beverages in hot weather. There are many different types, each with its own special flavour, and all belong to the intensely aromatic Labiatae family. The best known of all is spearmint (known variously as *Mentha viridis, M. spicata* and *M. crispa*) with its familiar piercing scent and green foliage. One strain of spearmint has smooth leaves, the other crinkly, but both have the same perfume. Applemint (*M. rotundifolia*) has round, greyish, apple-scented leaves. There is a variety with boldly marked cream and green leaves which is also widely known as variegated lemon balm (*M. rotundifolia variegata* or *M. officinalis variegata*). Eau-de-Cologne mint or bergamot ming (*M. piperita citrata*) is yet another variety, with highly perfumed foliage of a metallic green colour. Pennyroyal (*M. pulegium*) is a carpeting type of mint whose leaves have a strong peppermint odour. The true Mitcham peppermint (*M. piperita*) has small pointed leaves of purplish-tinted green which are fragrantly peppermint-scented.

The history of mint goes back to antiquity: it is mentioned in Greek mythology and in the Bible; the Romans introduced it to Britain, and it was familiar to Chaucer and Shakespeare. The ancient Greeks put it in their baths to refresh and strengthen the body. A decoction of mint was recommended as a wash for sore mouths. It was valued as a strewing herb, both for its sharp clean scent and its ability to drive away mice and insects. It helps prevent milk from curdling, and is good for the digestion.

Medicinally, peppermint is the most potent of all mints, the main constituent of peppermint oil being menthol. Peppermint tea has the effect of equalizing the circulation, and therefore tends to ease congestion. It is also a marked stimulant to the digestive tract and will allay nausea, sickness and vomiting. The oil is greatly

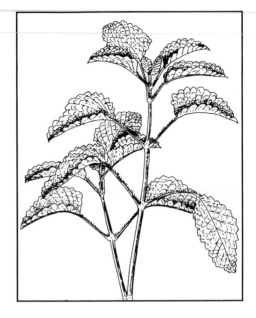

increased in peppermint plants if they are grown with stinging nettle. It has been found that production of the oil is retarded if peppermint plants are grown with camomile, but that the camomile itself will have a greater oil content.

Mints are perennial. They do best in rich, moist soil, but will also grow in poor sandy soil if the ground is fertilized occasionally. We have found that the flavour is stronger if the plants are grown in full sun, which increases their aromatic oil content, but they must be watered more frequently. Flower stems begin to shoot in late summer and autumn, producing clustered heads of tiny lipped flowers in various shades of mauve according to the type. The plants should be cut back to ground-level in winter. Sometimes mint is attacked by rust: if this happens, dig the plants up and start afresh with new stock in a different part of the garden. As mint seeds are very small and difficult to harvest, propagation is usually by root division in spring, summer and early autumn.

The leaves dry easily and retain all their flavour. For best results cut the stalks as the first flower-buds appear, and hang them in bunches or lay them on wire racks in a shady place. When they are ready, strip the leaves from the stems and store in airtight containers.

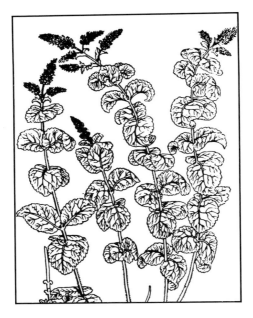

Balm (*Melissa officinalis*), another member of the Labiatae family, is similar to the mints and, like them, may be used in salads and drinks in hot weather. Often known as lemon balm, it has soft wrinkled foliage and a delicate lemon fragrance.

Balm flowers are loved by bees: in fact, the herb's Latin name of *Melissa* means bee. Bee-keepers have for centuries rubbed the inside of hives with balm leaves to prevent their bees from swarming. The name balm is an abbreviation of balsam, which it was once called because of its soothing sweetness.

Balm was used extensively for many ailments; a tea made from the leaves was recommended for feverish patients, helping to bring down high temperatures. It was also believed that balm would completely revive one, that it was a remedy for nervous disorders, helped the memory, assisted brain fatigue, sharpened comprehension, lifted the heart from depression and raised the spirits. There was once a Welsh prince who lived to 108 years who attributed his longevity to regularly drinking balm tea. On the farm, growing balm in the pastures is said to promote the flow of milk in cows. Also, a tea made with balm and marjoram has been given to soothe and strengthen cows after calving.

Balm is an evergreen perennial and like mint has a creeping

root system, but it is much easier to keep in check. It will grow in any soil, and likes a sunny position. In late summer the leafy stems rise to a height of 60 to 75cm (2 to 2½ ft), when the small white flowers appear on either side of their square stalks. In early autumn, ripe seed may be collected for sowing again immediately, or to store until the following spring. Propagation can also be carried out by root division in spring, summer and autumn. The foliage is dried in the same way as mint.

MINT ICE
(Serves 6)

This is one of the most refreshing sweets one could think of. My son Ian and his wife Elizabeth gave me the recipe—they nearly always have it made up and in a tray in the freezer in summertime.

250g (10 oz) raw sugar	green food colouring
500ml (16 fl oz) water	1 egg white, stiffly beaten
1 tablespoon finely chopped mint	mint leaves for decorating
juice of 4 lemons, strained	

Put the sugar and water into a saucepan on medium heat and stir until the sugar is dissolved. Take off the stove and stir in the mint. Cool. Add the lemon juice, and enough green food colouring to tint a pale green, then pour into a container and place in the freezing cabinet. When the mixture is beginning to set around the edges, scrape it into a bowl, beat well, fold in the stiffly beaten egg-white and pour back into the container to re-freeze. When set, serve in pre-chilled dishes. Garnish with mint leaves.

BALM TEA FOR STRENGTHENING THE MEMORY

An old recipe from *Lotions and Potions:*
One oz. balm to one pint of boiling water. Infuse for fifteen minutes—allow to cool. Drink freely. Sugar and lemon juice give this infusion a pleasant flavour.

SWISS BREAKFAST WITH MINT OR BALM
(Serves 1 or 2)

65g (2½ oz) rolled oats
250g (10 oz) plain yoghurt
juice of 1 orange
1 ripe apple, diced with
peel left on
40g (1½ oz) raisins

raw sugar or honey to taste
2 teaspoons chopped mint or
balm
2 teaspoons finely chopped
walnuts

Mix all ingredients together. If wished, serve with a little top milk or cream poured over.

COMPÔTE OF ORANGES WITH BALM
(Serves 6)

4 large sweet oranges
3 tablespoons cointreau
(optional)
2 teaspoons chopped balm or
spearmint

200g (8 oz) raw sugar
250g (8 fl oz) water
ice cream

Peel the skins very thinly from the oranges, making sure no pith is peeled off. Slice the peel into ½-inch-long sticks, or chop finely with a food chopper. Now remove all the pith from the oranges and discard it. Cut each orange into thin segments and place in a bowl. Add the cointreau and balm. Stir the sugar and water together in a saucepan, and simmer for 10 minutes. Pour half this syrup over the oranges. Chill. Put the cut-up orange peel into the rest of the syrup and simmer it for 10 minutes. Chill. Serve the compôte with ice cream or sour cream, pouring over it the finely cut peel in syrup.

PEPPERMINT TEA
(1 cup)

Pour 250ml (8 fl oz) boiling water on to 1 teaspoon dried peppermint leaves (or 2 teaspoons fresh leaves). Cover and infuse for several minutes. Strain and, if wished, sweeten with honey.

COOLING IDEAS FOR HOT DAYS

1. When making tea with your usual Indian tea, add a sprig of mint or balm to the pot before pouring on the boiling water.

2. Pick a generous bunch of eau-de-Cologne mint and arrange in a bowl of water: the strong perfume is refreshing and the hot atmosphere helps to draw it out.

3. Make lemon barley water flavoured with reviving balm to drink throughout the day for its healthful properties and delicious flavour. This barley beverage has long been known to benefit the kidneys. Our family recipe is simple: Put 2.5 litres (2 quarts) water, 100g (4 oz) raw sugar and 2 tablespoons pearl barley into a large saucepan and simmer with the lid on for 30 minutes. Strain, then add a few balm sprigs and the juice of 4 lemons. Cool, then chill.

4. Make mint ice-cubes by putting whole leaves or small sprigs of any of the mints into each section when filling ice trays with water for freezing. A hot and weary visitor is grateful for a drink from a frosty glass with fragrant mint ice-cubes tinkling in it.

5. When serving hot-weather drinks, place a leafy stalk of balm or mint in each glass.

6. Ice-cold peppermint tea is an excellent beverage to revive one on a hot day. Make a litre or so in the morning and chill it. Here is the recipe: pick a cupful of fresh peppermint leaves (or use 1 tablespoon dried leaves) and put into a bowl. Pour 625ml (1 pt) boiling water over, cover and infuse for 10 minutes. Strain, and sweeten with a little honey.

7. Chilled balm dressing is refreshing. To make it, stir 1 dessertspoon chopped balm or mint into 250ml (8 fl oz) yoghurt. Chill. For a sweet dressing add 2 teaspoons honey.

Herbs for all seasons

Bay

The bay laurel tree (*Laurus nobilis*) of the Lauraceae family is evergreen, and the leaves may be plucked in all seasons, including the middle of winter. Summer is a good time of the year to plant one or two from a nursery to make the most of growing time while the weather is still warm, for these trees are slow to begin with.

Bay laurel is sometimes confused with cherry laurel (*Prunus laurocerasus*), which is poisonous. It also has evergreen leaves, but the fruit is bright red and not dusky-black like that of bay laurel.

Bay-trees are native to the shores of the Mediterranean, and in warm climates they may reach a height of 15m (50 ft) or more; in cold areas they do not grow nearly as tall. When planting, find a sheltered sunny position for best results; in our temperate region we planted about twenty in an open field, and after ten years they had struggled to a height of 1.8m (6 ft), whereas in protected but sunny parts of the garden another two grew to 6m (20 ft) in the same length of time. Bay-trees are inclined to send up suckers around the base, and it is wise to cut these off to make a better looking tree. The only disease that seems to affect these trees is white wax scale, and this may be removed with soapy water and a scrubbing brush, or sprayed with white oil emulsion in late summer.

Bay-trees make excellent tub specimens and may be trained as standards on a central stem, with clipped, rounded tops. As the trees grow, they should be transferred to larger containers. I have seen a formal garden with a number of 1.8m (6 ft) bay-trees in spacious tubs placed at intervals in orderly pairs. They were all standards, with their foliage clipped into helmet-like shapes.

Bay leaves are dark-green and 8 to 11cm (3½ to 4½ in) long, narrow, firm and smooth with a warm, pungent aroma that is especially intense if the leaf is snapped, when the essential oil is released. The flowers are very small, appearing first as tiny hard buds opening to small creamy-white blossoms, followed by purple berries that go black and hard when dried. The tree remains dormant throughout winter, but early in spring new green leaves start shooting; when the shoots have hardened, after about eight weeks, 15cm (6 in) cuttings may be taken and planted in the garden.

Bay-leaves dry well, holding their perfume for years if properly stored; cut the branches before midday, then snip off the leaves, lay them in an airy, shady place (never in the sun), and when they are quite dry store them in an airtight container.

Victorious athletes and warriors, and poets too, of early Greece and Rome were crowned with wreaths of bay laurel leaves; Delphic priestesses are said to have made use of them; and for a long time the laurel was part of temple rites and ceremonies. In medicine, the oil from the leaves and berries was given in treating rheumatism, hysteria and flatulence, and it was used externally for sprains and bruises. A powder or infusion of the berries was taken to improve the appetite and to cure the ague. Culpeper, the seventeenth-century astrologer-physician, says it is a tree of the sun and 'resisteth witchcraft very potently . . .' He also says: 'The oil made of the berries is very comfortable in all cold griefs of the joints, nerves, arteries, stomach, belly, or womb . . .'

Herbs for all seasons

The special pungency of the leaves enhances the flavour of many foods, and besides being indispensable in most households, bay-leaves are used commercially in flavouring various types of canned and preserved fish, meat and vegetables. A bay-leaf is traditionally one of the four ingredients in a bouquet garni, the other herbs usually being a sprig each of thyme, marjoram and parsley: they are tied together and the bouquet is put into casseroles, soups and stews and removed after cooking. Bay-leaves on their own also flavour soups, stews and casseroles, as well as boiled, baked or steamed poultry, fish and meat; they go into marinades, and give a pleasing and unusual flavour to milk puddings. A few bay-leaves should also be added to a pot-pourri mixture.

AROMATIC BAKED FISH

whole fish, cleaned and scaled (about 400g (1 lb) for each person)
bay-leaves
vegetable oil

white wine
herb or vegetable salt
chopped tarragon
lemon slices, cut thinly

Lay the fish in a baking dish, place a bay-leaf in the cavity of each, pour oil and wine over and around the fish (1 tablespoon of each to every fish); sprinkle with salt and just a little of the tarragon, and arrange a couple of lemon slices on each fish. Bake in a pre-heated oven (185°C, 375°F) for about 45 minutes. During cooking, baste the fish with the pan juices from time to time. Serve hot.

BOILED SALT LAMB

Salt lamb or mutton when boiled like corned beef has a delicate flavour and texture. The aroma of bay-leaves and spices permeates the meat while cooking, and one medium-size to large leg is enough for three or four people for sandwiches or cold lunches for several days. Corned silverside or any other cut of corned beef may be substituted for the lamb or mutton in this recipe.

leg lamb or mutton,
1.5–2kg (4–5 lb)
2 bay-leaves
1 teaspoon black peppercorns

1 teaspoon ground ginger
1 teaspoon white vinegar
2 whole garlic cloves
1 tablespoon raw sugar

Place the meat in a large saucepan and cover with cold water. Add the rest of the ingredients, put the lid on and bring slowly to the boil, then turn the heat down a little and continue boiling gently for 2 hours. Turn the heat off and allow the meat to cool in the liquid. Drain and keep in a cold place.

SPICED WHOLE GRAPES

(Yield, 6 x 150g (6 oz) jars)

A delicious accompaniment to grills, baked meat, poultry, fish or curry.

800g (2 lb) seedless white grapes
400g (1 lb) raw sugar
150ml (5 fl oz) cider or white
vinegar
2 teaspoons mustard seed

1 teaspoon ground ginger
1 teaspoon ground allspice
2 bay leaves
25g (1 oz) powdered fruit pectin

Wash the grapes and remove the stalks. Place the sugar and vinegar in a saucepan and add the mustard seed, ginger, allspice and bay-leaves. Bring to the boil, then simmer gently with the lid off for 15 minutes, stirring at intervals. Remove the bay-leaves. Add the grapes, sprinkle in the pectin, bring to the boil again and simmer for a further 3 minutes, skimming off any foam and giving the mixture an occasional stir. Remove from the stove and allow to stand for 10 minutes, stirring frequently to prevent a film from setting on the top. Spoon into jars and seal down. Use within 4 weeks.

Elder

Elder (*Sambucus nigra*) is a small deciduous tree or large shrub, reaching a height of 4m (14 ft) and sometimes more: in summer it is covered with flat, filmy heads of creamy-white flowers which are soon followed by sprays of small shiny berries that turn from green to bright red, then purple and jet black. It grows wild in many parts of Europe, and is part of the folklore of a number of countries. The Anglo-Saxons called it Eldrun, which later became Hyldor and Hyllan tree. It belongs to the Caprifoliaceae family.

Danish legend connected this tree with magic, believing that in the branches dwelt a dryad, Hylde-Moer, the Elder-tree Mother, and that if one stood under the tree on Midsummer Eve one would see the King of Fairyland and all his train ride by. They also believed that a child's cradle should not be made of elder wood, for Hylde-Moer would come and pull the child's legs, giving it no peace until it was lifted out.

Russian peasants said that the compassionate spirit of the elder would drive away evil and also give long life. The Sicilians thought that sticks made of its wood killed serpents and drove away robbers, and in England it was held that the elder was never struck by lightning.

All parts of the elder are useful, it having once been called 'the medicine chest of the country people'. The close-grained white wood of old elder trees was cut and polished and made into butchers' skewers, shoemakers' pegs, needles for weaving nets, combs, mathematical instruments, and some musical instruments. The stems with pith removed made whistles and popguns for country boys. An infusion of the bitter leaves dabbed on the face is said to repel insects such as mosquitoes and flies; a decoction of the leaves sprinkled over delicate plants helps ward off aphis and caterpillars, and the leaves spread about where grain is stored drive away mice. The bark was used medicinally as a purgative as long ago as the time of Hippocrates, and a soothing ointment was made from the green inner bark. A tea made from the elder root was considered the best remedy for dropsy.

The uses of the flowers and berries are legion. An infusion of the dried flowers is excellent for soothing inflamed eyes. It is also most effective when patted on the skin to fade freckles: in fact this simple treatment is good for the complexion generally and, if kept up regularly, gives the skin a soft dewy bloom after a week or so. Elderflower tea is an old remedy for influenza, and taken every morning was also popular as a spring medicine to purify the blood; an ointment made from the flowers heals burns and chilblains; elderflower vinegar is a remedy for sore throats; the fresh flowers make a delicious wine; elderflower fritters are an unusual and delectable sweet; and elder blossoms give a muscatel flavour to gooseberry, apple or quince jelly when tied in a muslin bag and boiled in the fruit syrup for 3 or 4 minutes at the end of the cooking time.

Elderberries have been used for centuries to make elderberry wine, which has valuable medicinal qualities, including the alleviation of sciatic pains. It was common practice some years ago to adulterate cheap port with easily available elderberry juice so that it resembled tawny port (it was also then popularly believed that port cured rheumatic and neuralgic pain). Around 1899, investigations revealed that more expensive port without the addition of elderberries did not have the same effect! However, after extensive tests by some leading European doctors, it became accepted to recommend a dose of 30g of elderberry juice mixed with 10g of port wine for treating certain aches and pains. A cordial known as Elderberry Rob when taken hot before going to bed was a well-known cure for a cold; elderberry juice was used as a laxative and for colic. For preserves, the berries—which taste rather like black currants—flavour jams and jellies; or they may be used on their own to make elderberry jam or jelly, elderberry chutney and elderberry ketchup; the berries also give a distinctive sharp taste to fruit tarts and apple sauce.

To provide enough flowers and berries for use, grow at least three elder trees planted about 1.25m (4 ft) apart to make a small

thicket. They are hardy trees, fond of moisture, and prefer to grow in semi-shade. They should be cut back hard in winter. Strike cuttings of sprouting wood in spring or autumn in the open garden. (It has been noted that elders growing near compost heaps assist fermentation, and that humus under the trees is especially light.)

The flowers begin to appear in summer, so gather the heads when all the tiny buds on each pearly cluster are open, and do this by midday before the sun draws out too much of the flower's etheric substance. Lay the heads somewhere shady to dry—a sheet of paper in the linen cupboard is an excellent place to put them—and when they shrivel, looking like bundles of old, yellowed lace, remove them to make room for more fresh flowers. Store the dried flowers whole in airtight containers, or rub them off their frail stalks first (I prefer to leave them whole). Leave some flowers on the trees for using fresh, and to ensure that there will be some fruit later. When the jade-green berries appear, watch them ripen and pick them as they begin to turn reddish-purple. If left too long they will fall—or the birds will get there first! If it is not convenient to use the berries immediately, allow them to dry, following the same method as for flowers, and store in an airtight container for use later. They keep their flavour well, and may be used like dried currants in cakes and scones.

APPLE AND ELDERBERRY SAUCE

A mulberry-coloured piquant sauce to accompany hot or cold poultry or pork. Peel, core and slice 2 apples and place in a small saucepan with 2 sprays of ripe elderberries pulled off their stalks (fresh or dried), 3 tablespoons water and 1 tablespoon raw sugar. Cover, and simmer slowly until the apples are soft. Stir with a fork and turn into a dish. Serve hot or cold.

ELDERFLOWER TEA

An infusion of elderflowers for influenza. The addition of peppermint leaves to the elderflowers is said to be even more efficacious. Put 2 teaspoons dried elderflowers into a small teapot (not an aluminium one) and pour 1 cup boiling water onto them. Infuse for a few minutes, then strain into a cup. Do not add milk. If desired sweeten with honey.

VANILLA PRUNES IN ELDERBERRY WINE

A light port may be used in this recipe instead of the elderberry wine.

400g (1 lb) dessert prunes   250ml (8 fl oz) elderberry wine
½ vanilla bean

Put the prunes, broken pieces of vanilla bean and wine together in a
bowl and leave overnight or for some hours. Simmer in a saucepan
for 5 to 10 minutes. Serve chilled with sour cream or yoghurt.

ELDERFLOWER MILK JELLY
(Serves 4)

The elderflowers give a slight flavour of muscatel grapes to this jelly.

375ml (12 fl oz) milk   1 teaspoon powdered agar
1 tablespoon dried elderflowers   1 tablespoon water
1 tablespoon honey   1 tablespoon cream
ground nutmeg

Scald the milk with the elderflowers for 15 minutes, barely allowing
it to simmer. Strain the milk into a jug, pressing the juice gently out
of the flowers. Return the milk to a saucepan with the honey, and
reheat, stirring. Mix the agar and water together to a runny paste, add
to the milk, and simmer for 2 or 3 minutes. Take off the stove, stir in
the cream and pour into a wetted mould. Cool and chill. Unmould
and serve with a grating of nutmeg over the top. Agar sets the jelly:
the reason for refrigerating is that it tastes better if eaten cold.

ELIZABETHAN OR ELDERBERRY ROB

A recipe from *Lotions and Potions*, with a note that it is a very old recipe, well tried.
Put 5 pounds of washed, ripe elderberries with 1 pound of sugar into a saucepan and simmer until it is the consistency of honey. Strain and bottle. One or two tablespoonfuls to be taken at bedtime in very hot water. It is mildly laxative, will stop a cold and bring on a sweat. It relieves all chest troubles. A tablespoonful of whisky may be added if liked.

ELDERFLOWER OINTMENT

This healing ointment from *Lotions and Potions* requires 200g (8 oz) Vaseline (petroleum jelly) or pure lard, and 2.5l (4 pt) elderflowers without the thick stems.
Melt Vaseline or lard in a saucepan, add elderflowers. Allow to simmer for half an hour. While very hot, strain through muslin into small pots. Ready for use when cold. For heat lumps, bites, chapped hands, and also for cows' udders and teats. This ointment can be re-infused with rose petals or lavender to give it a pleasing perfume. It is especially good for chilblains.

APPLE AND ELDERBERRY TART

(Serves 6)

Pastry	*Filling*
150g (6 oz) unbleached or wholewheat pastry flour	400g (1 lb) apples, peeled, cored and sliced
1 teaspoon sugar	3 or 4 sprays ripe elderberries, fresh or dried
salt to taste	2 tablespoons raw sugar
100g (4 oz) butter or margarine	
1 egg, beaten	

The pastry   Sift the flour, sugar and salt into a bowl. Rub the butter in until the mixture resembles fine breadcrumbs. Add the egg and mix well. Roll the dough out thinly on a floured surface and line a greased 20 or 22cm (8 or 9 in) pie plate with it. Chill for 10 minutes or overnight.

The filling   Arrange the apple slices in the pastry case. Pull the elderberries off the stalks and scatter among the apple, then sprinkle sugar over the top. Place the tart in a moderate oven (175°C, 350°F) for 25 to 30 minutes, or until cooked. Serve hot or cold with cream, ice-cream or yoghurt.

ELDERBERRY WINE

1 gallon water, 3½ lb sugar, 7 pints elderberries, ½ oz ginger, a few cloves, 1 lb raisins. Boil the water and spices for 25 minutes. Add berries and raisins, boil for the same period. Let it stand until quite cold, then add the sugar. Leave for a month to work, and if you like, before bottling, add ¼ pint brandy and another 6 oz sugar to every gallon. May be used within 6 months if need be.

NELL HEATON   A Calendar of Country Receipts

FOR THE EYES

Make an infusion as above, but be sure to strain through fine muslin before using. Bathe the eyes several times a day with the lotion.

ELDERBERRY FACE LOTION

Pour 315ml (10 fl oz) boiling water onto 1 heaped tablespoon dried elderflowers. Cover and leave for at least 15 minutes, then strain the lotion into a screw-top jar and keep in the refrigerator. Instead of washing the face in the morning—or after having done so, if preferred—pour some elderflower lotion into a small bowl and, with a piece of cottonwool, pat it all over the face and neck and allow to dry on the skin. This quantity should be enough for one week if kept in a cold place and will stay fresh enough to use for this time.

ELDER MILK

Take two corymbs, or clusters, of elder blossoms, strip the flowers off and simmer them for ten minutes in a quart of milk. Then add a spoonful of semolina, heat up with sugar, a little salt, and two yolks of egg. Pour the milk into a bowl, and float on the top, when it is cold, little icebergs of the white of egg beaten up with sugar. Last of all, sprinkle sugar and cinnamon on the Elder Milk, which has the most delicate and chilly of flavours.

GEOFFREY GRIGSON   A Herbal of All Sorts

ELDERFLOWER FRITTERS
(Serves 4)

A slightly altered eighteenth-century recipe of John Nott, cook to the Duke of Bolton.

8 elderflower heads, washed
1 tablespoon orange-flower water
1 teaspoon ground cinnamon
150ml (5 fl oz) vegetable oil
1–2 tablespoons Superfine or
confectioner's sugar

BATTER
100g (4 oz) plain flour
salt to taste
½ teaspoon sugar
1 egg, separated
315ml (10 fl oz) milk

Place the elderflowers in a dish and sprinkle them with the orange-flower water and cinnamon. Make the batter by sifting the flour, salt and sugar together into a bowl, then drop in the egg yolk and some of the milk. Stir well and add the rest of the milk, beating until the batter is smooth. Whisk the egg white and fold it into the batter. Heat the oil in a frying pan. Take the elderflowers by their short stalks and dip them one at a time into the batter, covering them completely, then place them in the frying pan and cook until crisp and golden, turning them once. Drain on paper, sprinkle with sugar and serve hot with cream or yoghurt.

Lemon Verbena

Lemon verbena (*Lippia citriodora* or *Aloysia citriodora*) has such strongly perfumed leaves that when brushing past the foliage one is surrounded by a most refreshing light fragrance redolent of lemons. The histoi y of this tree does not go far back in European records, it having been introduced into England about 1784 from Chile. It belongs to the Verbenaceae family.

There is another verbena, the herb vervain (*Verbena officinalis*), which is found in herbal lore; it was esteemed by Hippocrates; the Druids used it as a cure for plague; magicians and sorcerers wove it into their spells and incantations; the Romans considered it a holy plant; it was also regarded as an aphrodisiac, and in Tudor times it was an ingredient in mixing love philtres. Vervain in appearance and scent is completely different from lemon verbena: it is a small perennial plant with spear-shaped leaves and small lilac flowers on long stems.

Although a newcomer to the herb garden compared with most herbs, lemon verbena is soon loved by all who know it. The tree grows 3 to 4.5m (10 to 15 ft) high in a sheltered, well-drained, sunny position. It is deciduous, and in winter the brittle, woody branches look quite lifeless—this is when the tree should be pruned back hard; pencil-thick prunings may be salvaged and cut into 15cm (6 in) lengths for striking in the garden. In severely cold conditions protect the roots of the tree with a mulch of leaf mould or grass cuttings. In spring, new shoots appear on the tree, and by midsummer it is thick with foliage on long, sappy branches spiked with plumes of pale-mauve flowerets.

Verbena leaves are light green, thin and pointed, about 10cm (4 in) long, with a slightly sticky feel and a pronounced citrus aroma. It is a simple matter to dry lemon verbena, and the tree responds to cutting. Gather an armful of leafy and flowering branches before midday and stack them at the back of a linen cupboard (the leaves perfume the linen while drying), or tie the branches together and hang them up on a shady veranda or in a dry shed. There seems to be no mildew problem with these leaves: they dry within a few days, when they may be stripped from their stems and stored.

The leaves, fresh or dried, are used in tisanes for reducing fevers, as a sedative, and for indigestion, as well as making an excellent cooling tea in very hot weather, either on their own or added to Indian tea. One or two fresh leaves placed on top of a rice pudding or baked custard before it goes into the oven impart a delicate flavour. One of the main uses for dried lemon verbena leaves is in pot-pourri, giving a light, piercing scent in contrast to the other sweet and spicy perfumes.

LEMON VERBENA RICE PUDDING

(Serves 4)

1½ tablespoons brown rice
1 tablespoon raw sugar
625ml (1 pt) milk

3 or 4 fresh lemon verbena leaves

Stir the rice, sugar and milk together in a buttered ovenproof dish and lay the verbena leaves on top. Place the dish on the middle shelf of a slow oven (150°C, 300°F) and bake for 2 to 2½ hours. During cooking, stir the pudding gently once or twice with a spoon, sliding the spoon under the skin from the edge. Serve hot or cold with cream or yoghurt and, if wished, serve some stewed fruit with it.

LEMON VERBENA TEA

(Serves 1)

Put 6 dried lemon verbena leaves into a teapot, pour 250ml (8 fl oz) boiling water onto them, infuse for a few minutes, then strain. Drink hot without milk. May be sweetened with honey.

ANTI-MOTH HERBS

Take a handful each of dried and crumbled lemon verbena, tansy, southernwood and rosemary. Mix with 1 tablespoon whole cloves and a piece of cinnamon stick. Sew into muslin bags and put into drawers and cupboards, or loop the bags onto coat-hangers.

Autumn

A HARVEST OF SPECIAL
FRUITS AND SEEDS
*crabapples cumquats quinces
rose hips anise caraway
coriander dill fennel*

When to bed the world are bobbing,
Then's the time for orchard robbing;
Yet the fruit were scarce worth peeling
Were it not for stealing, stealing.

LEIGH HUNT   Song of Fairies Robbing an Orchard

During the last weeks of summer some of the fruit in the orchard and herb garden is beginning to ripen. And when the first cool tang of autumn sharpens the air, mellow crabapples hang from leafy twigs in heavy cherry-like bunches; swollen knobbly quinces crowd japonica branches; full, flagon-shaped rose-hips glow red and gold amongst green foliage; and ripe cumquats shine temptingly on the tree like diminutive oranges. These special fruits should be harvested and concocted into healthful, delicious jams, jellies, conserves or syrups. With their richly gleaming colours of burgundy, amber, copper-pink and rose they make enchanting gifts when stored in attractive glass jars or ceramic pots and labelled: Whole Spiced Crabapples . . . Cumquat Marmalade . . . Quince Jelly . . . Rose-hip Syrup—their names alone are enticing.

As well as these autumn crops, the fruits or seeds of anise, caraway, coriander, dill and fennel should also be harvested for their particular and special uses. These plants are umbelliferous, like a number of other well-known culinary herbs—chervil and parsley for instance. When flowering, they are recognizable by their flat, spreading blossoms, each consisting of many tiny, perfectly bunched posies on straight, fragile stalks. Their complex flowers, although identical in form, differ widely from one another in size and colour, ranging from the small faded-lavender umbels of coriander to the large gold heads of fennel.

Anise, caraway, coriander, dill and fennel have one distinctive element in common: their flowers ripen into seeds abundant in oils with beneficial digestive properties. Whole or ground, these seeds help with the assimilation of starchy foods (such as pastries, breads, pasta and biscuits) and of certain vegetables tending to produce flatulence (such as cabbage, cucumber and onions), as well as helping us to digest stewed and baked fruit like apples, pears and quinces. They also complement root vegetables when cooked with them: one theory is that the seed's vital essence, drawn from the sun, air and light, is released during the cooking process, balancing the vegetable's heavy root substance that was moulded within the dark solidity of the earth.

Herbs for all seasons

Harvesting begins when the flower-heads start maturing in midsummer, and goes on into autumn. Some seed may drop . . . which reminds me of the almost forgotten practice in severe climates of 'mothering' the seeds that fall—that is, leaving them where they lie in the ground, covering and feeding them during winter. Seedlings that have been mothered, it is said, make the strongest and earliest plants, but in a very cold spring they should be protected or they may suffer.

Old herb books counsel one to sow all seed while the moon is waxing, and to harvest when it is waning. One of Tusser's 'Five Hundred Points of Good Husbandry' quoted in *The Herb Garden*, by Frances A. Badswell, reads:

> *Cut all things or gather, the moon on the wane,*
> *But sow in increasing, or give it its bane.*

If you are unable to grow your own plants for gathering the seed, you may buy it, in whole form or ground to a powder, in health-food shops and in most grocers' shops. If a recipe requires whole seed and you can find only the ground variety, use half the quantity instead.

Note how anise, caraway, coriander, dill and fennel resemble a human family with their mixture of friendly and antagonistic attitudes towards each other: anise, caraway and coriander all like growing near one another, even the germination of their seed being improved; fennel has an adverse effect on caraway; coriander, on the other hand, hinders the formation of fennel seed; and dill appears to grow happily with the entire clan.

■ ■ ■

In early autumn three bitter herbs of historic interest are blooming—namely rue, tansy and wormwood. Their foliage and flowers and the sharpness of their scent, all in their own way give contrast to the other herbs in the garden. They do not come into any particular group in this section, but a short description of each is appropriate.

Rue (*Ruta graveolens*) of the Rutaceae family, was often referred to by old writers as Herb-of-Grace. A perennial growing up to 90cm (3ft) tall, it has ornamental leaves like a bluish-green lace, and bright yellow flowers, green-tinted. Its unusual foliage enhances other plants in herbaceous borders. We have grown rue successfully in an urn on a terrace, nipping back the long stalks to encourage compact, dense growth. Rue was introduced to Britain by the Romans, who valued its medicinal properties. It is the bitterest of all herbs, and has no place in cooking. In companion planting, rue and basil dislike each other. It is an excellent herb to help repel flies, and a tea made of it, and sprinkled around liberally, kills fleas. Sow seed or propagate by root division in spring. Give the plant some sun during the day, and see that it is in a well-drained position.

Tansy (*Tanacetum vulgare*), one of the Compositae family, has another name, Buttons. A perennial, it grows to 90cm (3 ft) or more in height. Its ferny leaves grow thickly, and it makes a handsome bushy plant. The unusual flowers are clustered together on one head, looking like a bunch of small yellow buttons. Long stalks of the quaint blooms, together with the ferny leaves, look enchanting when bunched into a straight silver vase. A native of Europe, tansy was valued as a strewing herb because it helps repel flies. It has many medicinal uses, and certain old traditions are connected with it. Tansy cakes were eaten on Easter Day as a reminder of the bitter herbs eaten at the Feast of the Passover. The cakes were also considered very beneficial to health. The leaves only are generally used in food. They are finely chopped, but only a small amount of them, say half a teaspoon when chopped, for the aroma is stringently lemon and the flavour extremely bitter. In the garden, the foliage helps keep away many annoying insects such as moths and flies, although bees and other insects love the pollen-laden flowers. It is said that rubbing the surface of raw meat with tansy leaves will protect it from flies. Massaging a dog's coat with the leaves helps get rid of fleas. Tansy will grow in any position, and is propagated by root division in spring or autumn. Seed may be sown in spring.

Wormwood (*Artemisia absinthium*), another member of the Compositae family, and a perennial, grows into a small bushy shrub between 60 to 90cm (2 to 3 ft) high, with silky, serrated grey leaves. The tiny balls of lemongreen flowers are carried closely together vertically on long stalks in late summer and autumn. The leaves are almost as bitter as rue, and are not used in cooking, although they go into the making of absinthe. Wormwood was also sometimes employed by brewers instead of hops. The foliage has antiseptic properties, and was often used for fomentations.

Caution in placing wormwood near other plants in the garden is needed, because the root excretes a substance which inhibits the growth of plants, especially anise, fennel, sage and caraway, and rainwater falling from the leaves and onto the ground carries this element as well. A clump of wormwood bushes growing in the garden makes a restful silvery-grey picture. It is an excellent herb to help discourage cabbage moths, and when made into a tea and sprayed on the ground in autumn and spring will repel slugs and snails. The tea is supposed to rid domestic pets of fleas when rubbed into their coats. Wormwood likes a fairly shady situation. Sow seed in spring or autumn, or propagate by root division or cutting at these times.

Crabapples

Legend says that apples were the fruit on the Tree of Knowledge in the Garden of Eden. Magical apples grew on King Arthur's mystic isle of Avalon in Somersetshire, which lay:

> *Deep-meadow'd happy, fair with orchard-lawns*
> *And bowery hollows crown'd with summer sea . . .*

There are numerous mentions of apples in old Saxon herbal manuscripts.

The crabapple or wild apple (*Pyrus malus*) of the Rosaceae family, is ancestor to all cultivated varieties of apple-trees which have evolved through the centuries: cider apples, then dessert apples were developed from wild apples. As the tiny sharp-tasting red or yellow crabapples grew through grafting into larger, juicier and sweeter fruit, they were widely used as an aid to health in food. Fresh apples are rich in vitamins and organic acids and salts, and they are a help in digesting rich foods such as pork and goose— apple sauce has been a recognized accompaniment to these foods for centuries. It is well known that a raw apple eaten at night assists a sluggish system, and that apples are a natural mouth cleanser. There is an old saying:

> *To eat an apple going to bed*
> *Will make the doctor beg his bread.*

It was the custom in Elizabethan times to eat caraway seeds with roast apples, when a 'little saucerful' was served with them. There was already a broad variety of the fruit, and Shakespeare mentions crabapples, codlings, pippins, leathercoates, medlars, apple-johns, bitter-sweetings, pomewaters and costards. Even the smell of apples was supposed to be beneficial: Dr John Caius, physician to Queen Elizabeth I, advised his patients to 'smele to an old swete apple' when recovering strength after illnesses. Apples stuck with cloves, known as 'comfort apples', were a poor person's substitute for the rarer orange stuck with cloves for the rich. Apple cider is one of the oldest country drinks, and nearly every farmhouse made its cider each year. There are countless apple recipes in Mrs Leyel's *Gentle Art of Cookery*, from such familiar favourites as apple pie and apple fool to unusual recipes such as savoury apple soup and almond-crusted apples.

Because of their small size and sour taste there is not much demand for crabapples, and they are never seen in greengrocers' shops. However, there many delicious recipes in which they are used either on their own or with other food. In Ireland, crabapples are sometimes added to cider to impart a roughness, and in Shakespeare's day roasted crabapples were dropped into good brown ale:

> *When roasted crabs hiss in the bowl*
> *Then nightly sings the staring owl*

Love's Labour Lost, 5, II

Crabapple jelly is a rich ruby-red colour and has a hauntingly wild taste. Crabapples may be included in the ingredients for jam made with apples, blackberries, pears or quinces. Spiced crabapples are excellent to eat with meat and poultry. When roasting duck, goose or veal, surround the meat with a dozen or so ripe, raw crabapples during the last half-hour of cooking, then drain them on brown paper, dust with sugar and serve as an accompaniment.

It is intriguing to compare the form of an eating apple cut in half with that of a cherry-sized crabapple also cut in half. Observe how exactly their formation corresponds—even the fairy-like floribunda crabapple, which is no larger than a cherry stone, is a facsimile of a large apple.

Grow several varieties of crabapples for their different coloured flowers and fruit: all are spring blooming and summer-into-autumn fruiting. Crabapple trees are not difficult to grow, and they seem to remain free of disease. They thrive in almost any soil, and prefer a fair amount of sun. If the soil is very poor and sandy, however, for best crop results, dig in some fertilizer as the apples start forming. When planting in heavy ground, find a well-drained position and cultivate around the trees fairly frequently.

Unless the trees need shaping, pruning is not necessary, at least not for some years. As the crabapple becomes older, the gnarled satiny branches have great natural beauty, especially if left to grow in their own way. However, if you feel a tree needs thinning, do this in midwinter.

Some suggestions for planting are: *Malus purpurea eleyi*, which has wine-red single flowers and thick clusters of claret-coloured apples on long stems; *M.* 'Gorgeous', has beautiful white flowers tinged with carmine and brilliant scarlet and gold apples swinging in bunches; *M. spectabilis*, which is covered in red buds opening to semi-double pink flowers followed by russet fruit; *M. floribunda*, the Japanese crab, when in flower is a froth of palest shell-pink blossoms followed in autumn by hundreds of tiny golden fruit with a waxy sheen. Not so widely seen is the crabapple *M.* 'Golden Hornet', probably cultivated from the older *M.* 'Sovereign', which has sunny yellow apples and is well worth a place in the garden.

CRABAPPLE JELLY

crabapples	sugar
water	lemons

Wash the crabapples, cover them with cold water and bring to the boil. Simmer until the fruit is pulpy. Strain the fruit and liquid through a sieve or colander into a large bowl, allowing it to flow without pressing, although the pulp may be turned now and again with a spoon. Leave until the next day. When straining is finished, measure the liquid and allow 400g (1 lb) sugar and the juice of a lemon to every 625ml (1 pt). Put the strained crabapple liquid and lemon juice into a saucepan, bring to the boil and gradually add sugar, stirring well to dissolve it. Then boil rapidly until a little of the jelly sets on a saucer. Seal in clean, dry jars.

CRABAPPLE AND ROWAN JELLY

If you live in a cool climate you can grow a rowan-tree or mountain ash (*Sorbus aucuparia*) and use the edible red apple-like fruit. This recipe comes from Nell Heaton's *Calendar of Country Receipts*.

Soak the rowan berries in hot water for a day before you begin. Then add ⅓ of their weight in chopped crabapples. Simmer fruit with ½ pint water to every pound of fruit. Use the usual jelly procedure with the strained juice, adding a pound of sugar to each pint, and a little lemon juice. This astringent jelly is good with meat.

WHOLE SPICED CRABAPPLES

ripe, firm crabapples	black peppercorns
sugar	whole cloves
white vinegar	cinnamon stick

Wash the crabapples and remove the stalks. Put the fruit into a large saucepan, cover with cold water and bring to the boil, then simmer gently until the apples are tender but still hold their shape—10 to 15 minutes. Take off the stove and measure the fruit with the liquid in a measuring jug. To every 625ml (1 pt) of crabapples and liquid allow 400g (1 lb) sugar and 2 tablespoons vinegar. Drain off the liquid into a saucepan, reserving the fruit until later. Add the sugar, vinegar, a few peppercorns, several cloves and a piece of cinnamon stick to the liquid in the saucepan. Bring to the boil, stirring well to dissolve the sugar. Lower the heat and boil slowly until the syrup has become reduced somewhat—about 1 hour. Add the reserved crabapples and cook gently for a further 20 to 30 minutes, skimming off any foam. Fill clean, dry jars with the crabapples and spicy syrup. Seal down.

CLOVE APPLE OR APPLE POMANDER

The spicy aroma of pomanders wafts through cupboards and drawers, helping to keep moths away in a fragrant and efficient manner. This recipe is for a full-sized apple, so while they are fresh and plentiful make a clove apple instead of a clove orange. They are both prepared in the same way. First of all, make sure the fruit is absolutely fresh and unblemished, then press cloves all over it, starting from the stalk and going round the apple until it is covered. For a hanging pomander, now press a staple into the top. Mix together on a square of tissue paper 2 teaspoons orris root powder and 2 teaspoons ground nutmeg. Roll the clove apple in this, then twist the paper lightly together round it and store in a dark cupboard for a few weeks. After the apple pomander has hardened, remove from the cupboard and shake off any excess powder. Thread a pretty ribbon through the staple and tie in a loop.

Kumquats

The uncommon kumquat-tree with its brilliant sour fruit originated from eastern Asia and is a distinct species of the citrus family, not a hybrid.

An English traveller of the nineteenth century, Robert Fortune, introduced the first kumquat-tree into Europe in 1846, and in many botanical books the genus bears his name. There are two species: Nagami, with oval fruit (*Fortunella margarita*) and Marumi, with round fruit (*F. japonica*). A green-and-white leaved kumquat has Marumi-type round fruit.

Sliced kumquats can be made into a pleasant sharp marmalade; left whole the fruits make a luscious translucent preserve to accompany curries, baked meat and poultry; or the preserve may be eaten as a dessert with yoghurt or cream. A curaçao can also be made from kumquats soaked in gin. An entirely different use for this fruit was thought of by my son Ian and his wife Elizabeth, who made fragrant kumquat pomanders into pendants. They threaded hardened clove-studded kumquats on a long leather ribbon to wear round their necks, and gave them to friends as well.

Kumquat-trees make attractive tub specimens and may be kept for many years in containers if they are looked after: train the tree to a 90cm (3 ft) standard, and keep trimmed to a round shape so that when in fruit the foliage is almost covered by the small golden balls.

The trees are ornamental when planted in the garden, and they soon grow nearly as large as orange-trees. The leaves are firm, narrow and pointed, and release a refreshing scent when crushed. In spring, perfumed waxy flowers resembling orange-blossom appear. There are several crops of the juicy, thin-skinned fruit: the first harvest ripens in autumn and by midwinter the bright globes prolifically festoon almost every inch of polished greenery, while the preserving pan is in constant use.

Grow kumquat-trees in a sunny position with good drainage, and water them regularly, especially in dry weather. Feed three times a year with citrus fertilizer, using about 1.6kg (4 lb) at each application, and cultivate lightly around the surface-growing roots. Like all citrus fruits, cumquats are susceptible to white wax scale, but this may be rubbed off with soapy water and a scrubbing brush. In companion planting it is said that citrus trees like the protective influence of oak, guava and rubber trees.

SPICED WHOLE KUMQUATS

1.6kg (4 lb) ripe kumquats
625ml (1 pt) white wine vinegar

1.2kg (3 lb) sugar
a few 5cm (2 in) pieces of
cinnamon bark

Prick the kumquats with a darning needle, put them in a saucepan, cover with water and bring to the boil. Simmer gently until soft, then drain them and throw away the water. Put the vinegar and sugar in a separate saucepan and boil for 20 minutes. Add the kumquats and cinnamon bark and cook for a further 10 minutes. Spoon the kumquats into jars, then pour the amber-coloured syrup over the fruit, seeing that there is a piece of cinnamon in each jar. Seal down. For kumquats in sweet syrup, make in the same way, but to 1.6kg (4 lb) kumquats allow 1.25 litres (1 quart) water instead of the white wine vinegar, and 2kg (5 lb) sugar instead of 1.2kg (3 lb); also, omit the cinnamon bark.

KUMQUAT MARMALADE

Wash 1.2kg (3 lb) ripe kumquats and slice them into an enamel or earthenware bowl. Add 3.75 litres (6 pt) water and allow to stand overnight. Transfer to a preserving pan and simmer until the fruit is tender. Add the juice of 3 lemons, then gradually stir in 2.4kg (6 lb) sugar. Boil until a little sets on a saucer. Fill clean, dry jars and seal when cold.

MORETTA'S KUMQUAT LIQUEUR

24 to 30 kumquats	405ml (13 fl oz) brandy
405ml (13 fl oz) gin	800g (2 lb) sugar

Wash the kumquats, then prick each one all round with a clean knitting-needle. Place the fruit in a screw-top jar together with the gin, brandy and sugar. Screw the lid on, and allow to stand for about five days, turning daily until the sugar is dissolved. Wait at least six months before using.

KUMQUAT POMANDERS FOR PENDANTS

Select ripe, unblemished kumquats, clipping them carefully off the tree so as not to tear the fine skin. Stick each one full of cloves, starting from the stalk end and going round until the kumquat is completely covered. Roll in a mixture of orris root powder and ground cinnamon (1 teaspoon of each to every cumquat), press a small staple lightly into the top, wrap in tissue paper and put away in a dry, dark place for two weeks. When hardened, thread a length of thin leather strapping or narrow velvet ribbon through the staple, pressing it firmly down into the kumquat.

Quinces

The Japanese flowering quince, a most attractive shrub, reaches a height of 1.5 to 1.8m (5 to 6 ft). It used to be known botanically as *Cydonia*, but is now *Chaenomeles*, from the Greek *chainein*, to split, and *meles*, apple. Many of the species come from Japan, hence the name japonica often given to the quince. It is a deciduous shrub and it flowers in late winter and spring. The showy fruit appears in summer and is fully ripe for preserving in early autumn. Like the fruit of the better known European quince, *Pyrus cydonia*, it is too hard to eat raw.

The japonica I most vividly remember grew as an impenetrable hedge around the kitchen garden of our first farm at Exeter in southern New South Wales. Planted by a previous owner, an Englishwoman, it leapt into a cheerful screen of burning scarlet flowers while the weather was still bleak and cold. In time, every thorny branch was clustered with miniature quinces, and people would tell me how the Englishwoman used to make jelly with the fruit, but in my youthful ignorance I merely thought it must have been an eccentric whim, and let them fall on the ground.

Later on I was to see Margaret Davis create ethereal flower pictures with two or three branches of blooming japonica and, later still, I learnt how to make jelly from the fruit.

There are several types, with flowers of different colours, to grow singly, in clumps or as a hedge. *Chaenomeles nivalis* has pure white flowers: *C. rubra grandiflora* has rich red blooms; *C.* 'Scarlet Double' produces scarlet flowers; and *C.* 'Winter Cheer' has vivid orange flowers.

Flowering quinces thrive in any soil and position, but prefer good drainage and part sun. Although they will tolerate dry conditions, for best results keep them watered during hot, dry summers. Prune old wood from the centre of the bush after flowering. For propagating, take root cuttings or hardwood cuttings in early winter and plant in open ground.

Herbs for all seasons

QUINCE JELLY

Cut well-washed quinces into small pieces (do not peel or core). Put
into a preserving pan, cover with cold water and bring to the boil.
Simmer until pulpy, then strain through a jelly bag for some hours or
overnight. Measure the juice and heat it in the pan. Gradually add
400g (1 lb) sugar to every 625ml (1 pt) of quince liquid and boil until
a little sets on a saucer, about 20 minutes. A few rose-geranium
leaves to impart a subtle fragrance may be added during the last 10
minutes of boiling and removed when the jelly comes off the stove.
Fill clean dry jars with the liquid. Seal when cold. Serve the jelly with
hot or cold poultry, fish and meat; or spread thickly
on buttered scones.

Rose hips

Our ancestors knew that rose hips were a valuable source of nourishment, and many people today are also aware of their value. Jams, jellies and syrups of rose hips were part of the store cupboard of long ago in Britain, Norway, Sweden, Germany, France and Russia; and as well as being used in preserves, rose hips were included in tart fillings and sauces. Sauce Eglantine, made from the red hips of the briar rose, was frequently served at Balmoral in Queen Victoria's time: the seeds were first removed from the hips and a sweet purée made with a little lemon juice added. Rose hips are extremely rich in vitamin C, and they also contain vitamins A, E, B and P. Rose-hip syrup, found in health food, grocery and chemist shops today, is a preventive against colds and is especially recommended for babies and young children. Rose seeds are known to be helpful to the kidneys, and when these are dried together with the pod, which is sliced, they are made into a tea which is carefully strained of the seeds before it is served.

In autumn, many rose bushes are bearing red and gold fruit, the most colourful and best shaped being those of the old roses. Of all the roses we have grown, the most prolific for both flowers and hips is the Apothecary's Rose (*Rosa gallica officinalis*). Some wild roses have these brilliant hips too. Before cooking, unless the juice only is used, remove the hairy seeds from inside the fleshy berry, for they can cause internal irritation.

ROSE HIP JELLY

When rose hips ripen, pick them before they go soft and make this fragrant jelly for spreading on thin bread and butter; or use it as a delicate sauce for ice cream, or to accompany poultry or fish. Pick and wash ripe, firm hips, cut in half and place them in a saucepan. Cover with water, put the lid on and simmer gently until the fruit is soft—about 1 hour. Strain the liquid through a sieve or colander which has been lined with muslin or gauze to prevent any rose-hip particles falling through. Measure the liquid and return it to the saucepan with 400g (1 lb) sugar and the juice of a lemon to every 625ml (1 pt) of rose-hip liquid. Simmer until a little jelly sets on a saucer. Pour into clean, dry jars and seal down.

ROSE HIP SYRUP

Pick bright orange hips, crush, put into boiling water (1½ pints per pound). Bring back to boil, stand for 15 minutes, strain through muslin. Bring solid mass to boil again in ½ pint of water, stand again for 15 minutes and strain. Mix juices, reduce by slow boiling to a pint per pound. Sweeten and bottle. Don't keep overlong.

NELL HEATON   A Calendar of Country Receipts

ROSE HIP AND APPLE CHEESE

(Yield, 6 x 185ml (6 fl oz) jars)

A fruit cheese is a preserve of sweetened fruit pulp which becomes thick and almost solid after cooking.

900g (2¼ lb) apples
50g (2 oz) red rose hips
315ml (10 fl oz) fresh orange juice

150ml (5 fl oz) water
800g (2 lb) raw sugar

Wash and chop up the unpeeled and uncored apples. Slice the rose hips and tie them in a muslin bag. Put the apples and rose hips into a preserving pan with the orange juice and water and cook over low heat with the lid on until the apples are soft and pulpy. Remove the bag of rose hips and discard. Press the apples through a sieve and measure the purée. For every 400g (1 lb) allow 400g (1 lb) of sugar. Put the pulp and the sugar into the pan, and cook over medium heat, uncovered, until very thick—about 1 hour. Stir frequently to prevent burning or sticking. Spoon into jars while hot. Serve this preserve with all kinds of meat, or on warm new bread, fresh scones or hot buttered toast.

ROSE HIP AND APPLE SNOW

(Serves 6)

500g (1¼ lb) apples
2 tablespoons water
1 tablespoon lemon juice
2 tablespoons clear honey

185ml (6 fl oz) rose hip syrup
(home-made or purchased)
3 tablespoons gelatine
4 tablespoons very hot water
2 egg whites

Peel, core and slice the apples into a saucepan. Add the water, lemon juice and honey, and cook until the apples are soft. Take the saucepan off the stove, add the rose hip syrup and beat with a rotary beater. Blend the hot water with the gelatine and incorporate into the apple and rose hip mixture. Whip the egg whites until stiff, fold into the apples and place in the refrigerator to set. Pile the mixture into glasses and serve topped with cream or ice cream and a scattering of crystallised rose petals or crushed nuts.

Anise

Anise (*Pimpinella anisum*), an annual that is native to Middle Eastern countries, was cultivated long ago by the ancient Egyptians, who valued its medicinal properties and culinary uses. It was also known by the early Greeks and Romans.

This herb was introduced to different parts of Europe during the Middle Ages, when its reputation spread rapidly. The plants are cultivated mainly for the pungent fruit. Some commercial uses for the seed are in the making of cough lozenges, in some curry blends, and in the liqueur Anisette, which if mixed with a little hot water is said to help relieve chest congestion. Also, Anisette stirred into iced water in summer makes a refreshing pick-me-up.

A visiting scientist once told us how, when in America on a research program, she was suffering badly from flatulence because of the recent removal of her gall-bladder, and no medicine prescribed for her could help. One day she suddenly recalled an old remedy for wind from her native Germany, a seed tea made with aniseed, caraway seed and fennel seed. After making the tea and taking it regularly, she was soon cured of her discomfort.

Aniseed's healing properties for the digestion are especially good for young children and help a nursing mother in the secretion of milk. Aniseed tea mixed with warm milk and honey and given at bedtime makes a soothing drink for the restless child. Small additions of anise powder helps the very young to digest their first solid foods.

Anise plants like sunshine and warmth, and will not always grow in cold, damp areas. In our temperate climate we have grown anise all the year round, making two sowings, one in spring and another in autumn. Seed may be sown where the plants are to remain, in light soil in a well-drained, sunny position near caraway and coriander. When seedlings appear, thin them to 30cm (12 in) apart:

the feathery-leaved plants grow to 45cm (18 in) high, with lacy, creamy white flowers. When the fruit is ripening, pick off the heads and lay them in boxes, or on fine racks, to dry, then shake out the tiny brown seeds and keep them in labelled airtight containers. They have a warm licorice flavour.

Another type of anise, called star anise, comes from a small tree (*Illicium anisatum*) that is a native of China and has the same digestive properties as the umbelliferous kind.

ANISEED
(1 cup)

For flatulence and sleeplessness, take after meals or on going to bed. Measure 470ml (15 fl oz) water into a saucepan (not an aluminium one) and bring to the boil. Add 1 teaspoon aniseed, put on the lid, lower the heat and simmer for 15 minutes. Strain and drink hot or warm. (The liquid reduces during simmering.) Sweeten with honey if wished. Hot milk may also be mixed with the tea.
If you can obtain only the ground seed, use half the quantity of seed and one-quarter less water. The method is slightly different in this case: bring the water to the boil and pour it directly on to the powdered seed. Stir well and, if wished, strain through muslin.

Anise

SEED TEA

(3 small cups)

For flatulence, sip a teacupful three times a day after meals. Using 625ml (1 pt) water and 1 teaspoon each of aniseed, caraway seed and fennel seed, make in the same way as aniseed tea. Keep the left-over tea covered in a cool place, and heat the quantity required each time. If you want to substitute ground seed, follow the quantities and instructions given above for aniseed tea.

SPICY FRUIT CAKE

(Weight when cooked, about 1.6kg (4 lb))

200g (8 oz) shelled, halved almonds
3 tablespoons rosewater
100g (4 oz) each of these glacé fruits: pineapple, pears, quinces, prunes, apricots, red cherries
100g (4 oz) mixed peel
100g (4 oz) sultanas
100g (4 oz) seeded raisins
175g (7 oz) wholewheat pastry flour
25g (1 oz) self-raising flour
salt to taste
2 teaspoons ground coriander seed
1 teaspoon ground aniseed
1 teaspoon ground cinnamon
1 teaspoon ground nutmeg
200g (8 oz) butter
75g (3 oz) raw sugar
175g (7 oz) clear honey
5 eggs
juice and grated rind of ½ lemon
150ml (5 fl oz) rum, brandy, whisky or orange juice

Soak the almonds in rosewater (which is available from delicatessens or chemist shops). It is preferable to leave them overnight, but soak for at least 2 hours. Prepare a 20cm (8 in) square or round tin by lining the sides and bottom with two layers of brown paper and one layer of buttered parchment paper, allowing a good 5cm (2 in) collar and pushing the paper well into the corners or sides of the tin. Prepare the glacé fruit and mixed peel by cutting the large pieces into big chunks and halving the smaller pieces, then put them into a bowl with the sultanas and raisins. Drain off and discard any rosewater that the almonds have not soaked up, then add the almonds to the fruit. Sift all the dry ingredients together into another bowl, mixing a small portion through the fruit and nuts to separate them.

Cream the butter and sugar, add the honey and beat until smooth. Beat in the eggs one at a time, then the lemon juice and grated rind. Fold in the sifted spiced flour, then the fruit, and lastly the spirits or orange juice. Spoon the cake mixture into the prepared tin, pressing the batter well into the corners and smoothing the top. Bake in a slow oven (150°C, 300°F) for 2 to 2½ hours. Let the cake cool in the tin for 30 minutes, then turn on to a wire tray and peel off the paper. When the cake is quite cool, wrap it in cheesecloth, sprinkle with rum, brandy, whisky or sherry and store in a sealed container.

Caraway

Caraway (*Carum carvi*) is a biennial plant indigenous to Europe, parts of Asia, India and North Africa. It grows up to 60cm (2 ft) high, has finely cut, ferny leaves like the foliage of carrots, and white summer-blooming flowers that are followed by brown sickle-shaped fruit containing aromatic oils. The leaves also contain a valuable essence and have been included in spring soups for their flavour and goodness; a teaspoon or two of finely chopped leaves of caraway also flavours salads and cooked vegetables. The roots are thick and tapering like those of carrots and parsnips, and may be cooked and eaten in the same way.

Caraway's qualities were recognized by the ancient Egyptians and the early Greeks and Romans. The herb was widely known in the Middle Ages and was popular in Shakespeare's day. Like aniseed, the fruit has been used for centuries in breads and cakes, and with baked fruit, especially roast apples. In *Henry IV Part 2*, Falstaff is invited by Justice Shallow to eat a 'pippin and a dish of caraways'. Caraway-seed cake is as traditional in England as apple pie or gingerbread. In Germany the seed is used extensively in cabbage dishes, with root vegetables, in bread and in cheeses. The oil expressed from the seeds goes into the liqueur Kummel. In Scandinavian countries the seed flavours nourishing black breads. Because caraway was said to prevent lovers from straying, it was once an essential ingredient in love potions. The seed baked in dough is given to pet pigeons to keep them, it is said, from wandering away.

The digestive properties of the fruit are identical with those of aniseed. However, the flavour is stronger, and reminiscent of the zesty bite of orange or lemon peel. Caraway seeds, and the leaves and root also, are especially good for assisting the activity of the glands, increasing the action of the kidneys, and generally being an excellent 'house cleaner' for the body. These qualities are described by Maria Geuter in *Herbs in Nutrition*:

. . . It is best pictured as a kind and loving caretaker who looks after the house, unlocks the doors of the gland, climbs right to the top and kindles the light in the brain, cleans the windows of the eyes to give a better view of the world, ventilates the rooms, burning any fuel however wet or cold. It also regulates the water system, cares for the comfort of the organism, and is altogether like a good old factotum . . .

A number of people are prejudiced against caraway seed, having eaten seed cake as children and disliked it. I was talking about this one day with a friend and we agreed that while caraway in sweet food has an overpowering taste for some, in savoury food it takes on a different character and is less assertive. Try the seed with baked or fricassee'd onions, in potato dishes, with a little water and butter when cooking turnips and carrots, in cabbage dishes and in breads. Mix caraway seed with cheese, and sprinkle sparingly over apples or pears before baking them.

When growing caraway, plant the seed in spring or autumn. Sow in a well-drained, sunny position where the plants are to remain, thinning out the seedlings later if necessary, and grow near anise and coriander. After the plants have flowered, and when the fruit has begun to mature, pick off the heads and lay them in boxes, or on fine racks, to dry out. When ready, shake out the seeds and store in labelled airtight containers.

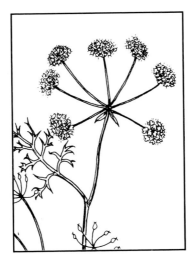

CARAWAY SEED TEA
(1 cup)

For flatulence, to be taken after meals. Make this in the same way as aniseed tea (page 119).

POTATO CARAWAY CREAM
(Serves 4)

A warm and comforting dish in cooler weather, and an excellent accompaniment to grills, rissoles or meat loaf. When quantities are doubled it may be eaten as a light main meal with poached smoked fish, or with slices of cold cooked meat.

400g (1 lb) potatoes	freshly ground pepper
25g (1 oz) butter or vegetable margarine	315ml (10 fl oz) hot milk
a few caraway seeds	1 egg yolk
herb or vegetable salt to taste	chopped parsley

Boil the potatoes in their skins until nearly cooked but still firm. Remove the skins and slice the potatoes thickly. Melt the butter or margarine in a heavy shallow pan and add the potato slices, turning them gently over medium heat until golden. Sprinkle with the caraway seeds, salt and pepper, then pour in the hot milk. Turn the heat down very low, place the lid on the pan, and simmer for 15 to 20 minutes, or until the potatoes are soft but not broken up. Just before serving, whisk a few tablespoons of hot liquid from the pan into the egg yolk and stir into the potatoes, turning the heat off at the same time to prevent curdling. Sprinkle liberally with chopped parsley just before serving.

Herbs for all seasons

BRANDIED CARAWAY APPLES

(Serves 4)

4 apples
2 teaspoons caraway seed
1 tablespoon seedless raisins

2 or more tablespoons clear
honey
65ml (2 fl oz) brandy or orange
juice

Cut the apples in half, core them and arrange in an oven-proof
serving dish. Place some of the caraway seed, raisins and honey on
each half. Pour the brandy or orange juice over and around the apples
and bake them in a moderate oven (175°C, 350°F) until soft—45 to
60 minutes—basting once or twice during cooking with the honey
and brandy sauce from the dish. Serve hot or warm with cream,
sour cream or yoghurt.

Coriander

Coriander (*Coriandrum sativum*) grew first in southern Europe and the Near East. The Egyptians made use of it; Hippocrates and other Greek physicians employed it in their medicines; and for the Hebrews it was one of the bitter herbs at the Feast of the Passover. The colonizing Romans first introduced coriander to Britain, where nowadays it is an established indigenous herb.

The fruit when mature is one of the most deliciously aromatic of all seeds. However, when still green and unripe, the seeds, like the leaves, have a strange raw odour, similar to that given off by a green beetle often found in gardens and citrus orchards. In fact, the name coriander is derived from the Greek *koris*, which means bug. The leaves are used extensively in cooking, especially in Peru, India, Thailand, Vietnam and Egypt, and are frequently laid on spicy Lebanese dishes as a garnish. ✳

The digestive action of the seed is particularly effective with carbohydrates, and has been used traditionally, whole or ground, in breads and cakes: coriander's use in cornbread, or polenta, goes back to the early Romans. The fragrant seed was once popular in confectionary and, I remember, formed the aromatic centre of a candy rainbow-ball popular with children.

Coriander seed is excellent to use when making pickles; whole or ground it flavours certain meat and fish dishes, as well as soups, stewed or baked fruits, and some salads. Its gentle aroma, which rounds out the fieriness of some other spices, makes it an important ingredient in curry blends.

Coriander is an annual and may be planted in spring or autumn, the seed being sown where the plants are to remain. The seed stays fertile for at least 5 years, and germinates quickly. Choose a well-drained, sunny place, and grow near dill and fennel. Coriander also likes the company of chervil. Plants grow up to 75cm (2½ ft) high, with finely cut, feathery foliage. The pale-mauve umbelliferous flowers are small and delicate looking, and

This spice gives ball-park hut dogs their distinctive taste FDW truva 4.96

* per LATIN fresh coriander leaf = cilantro

the round to oval seeds that follow turn from bright green to beige as they mature. Ripening heads should be cut and placed in boxes, or on fine racks, to dry, then the seeds removed and stored in labelled airtight containers.

CORIANDER YOGHURT-CHEESE PIE
(Serves 8)

Low in calories, this pie is cool and light to eat, with a delightful combination of flavours.

Crumb crust
200g (8 oz) graham crackers
200g (8 oz) butter or margarine
4 teaspoons ground
coriander seed

Topping
1 x 375g (15 oz) can whole figs
in syrup
2 teaspoons arrowroot or
cornstarch

Filling
400g (1 lb) cottage cheese
250g (10 oz) yoghurt
200g (8 oz) powdered skim milk
2 tablespoons boiling water
1 packet unflavoured gelatine
50g (2 oz) honey
2 teaspoons rosewater

The crust
Crush the graham crackers to fine crumbs with a rolling-pin. Melt the butter, mix with the crumbs and ground coriander in a bowl and press into a 25cm (10 in) pie-plate. Chill.

The filling
Press the cottage cheese through a sieve into a bowl, add the yoghurt and skim milk and beat till smooth. Pour the boiling water on to the gelatine, stirring until clear, then add it, with the honey and rosewater, to the cheese mixture. Beat once more, then pour into the prepared shell and chill overnight, or place in the freezing compartment of the refrigerator until firm—about 1 hour.

The topping
Drain the figs. Pour the syrup into a small saucepan, reserving about 2 tablespoons to blend with the arrowroot. Place the figs on the pie, heat the syrup, add the blended arrowroot and stir until thick and clear, then pour over the figs. Allow to cool and serve with cream.

CORIANDER CORNBREAD

(Serves 4 to 6)

Serve hot with roast meat, especially chicken, or with casseroles. When cold, this cornbread is excellent with butter, and honey or golden syrup.

1 egg
65ml (2 fl oz) vegetable oil
250ml (8 fl oz) milk
125g (5 oz) unbleached or
wholewheat flour
125g (5 oz) finely ground
cornmeal

3 teaspoons baking powder
1 tablespoon raw sugar
salt to taste
½ teaspoon ground coriander
seed

Beat the egg, oil and milk together in a bowl. Sift into this mixture the flour, cornmeal, baking powder, sugar, salt and coriander. Fold together lightly. Spoon the batter into a greased loaf tin which is at least 8cm (3 in) deep and measuring about 20 by 10cm (8 by 4 in). Bake in a medium to hot oven (175–190°C, 350–375°F) for 25 to 30 minutes. Test the centre with a skewer before turning out and cutting into slices.

Dill

Dill (*Anethum graveolens*) is native to the Mediterranean regions and southern Russia. It was familiar to the ancient civilizations of Greece and Rome, it is referred to in early Saxon manuscripts, and it was often mentioned by writers in the Middle Ages. The name dill is derived from the Norse *dilla*, to lull, showing how old is its reputation as a soothing herb. It was also considered a charm against witchcraft in the Middle Ages, and was burned to drive away thunderous clouds and sulphurous fumes.

When growing, dill looks remarkably like fennel, but the flowers, although yellow, are smaller, and the foliage is finer and a deeper green in colour. The single stalks spring up to a height of 90cm (3 ft), and without the bushy habit of fennel.

Medicinally, only the seeds of dill are valued because of their oil content. In cooking, both leaves and seed have a wide use, and the flavour imparted to the dish is almost the same except that with the seeds it is stronger. While aniseed, caraway seed and fennel seed all have a similar sweetish pungency, the taste of dill seed is different: it is astringently aromatic, and may be used instead of the other seeds if preferred.

The dry scent of the leaves is pleasing to most people, and may be substituted as a variation in dishes where you would use parsley, mint, basil or tarragon. Finely chopped dill leaves are particularly good in creamed potatoes, or in white sauce, cottage or cream cheese, fish dishes, omelettes, chicken dishes, salads, soups, vegetables and vinegars.

In appearance, dill seed is flat and light brown: it improves the flavour and digestibility of such differing foods as soups, pickles, fruit pies, seafood, cheese dishes, many salads and certain vegetables.

Dill is an annual, and seed should be sown in spring in a sunny place where the plants are to stay. In climates that do not have a severe winter, a second sowing in autumn is also possible. The leaves dry well, with a good green colour and excellent flavour, and cutting of them may be done throughout the summer. Hang the stems in an airy, shady place and, when brittle, crumble off the leaves and store in an airtight storage jar. Seeds are collected and stored in the same way as aniseed (page 119).

BROWN RICE AND DILL-SEED SALAD
(Serves 4)

400g (1 lb) brown rice
8 tablespoons cold pressed
vegetable oil
1 tablespoon apple cider vinegar
(or 2 tablespoons lemon juice)
1 clove of garlic, finely chopped

1 tablespoon dill seed
salt to taste
1 tablespoon capers
1 tablespoon husked sunflower
seeds
1 tablespoon kelp meal

Cook the rice in plenty of boiling salted water until tender—about 35 minutes. Turn into a sieve and run cold water through the grains to separate them, then drain well and transfer to a bowl. Stir the oil, vinegar and garlic together and pour onto the warm rice, tossing well. Fold in all the other ingredients and toss again. Chill and serve.

DILL SEED AND PUMPKIN SOUP
(Serves 4 to 6)

800g (2 lb) peeled pumpkin
2 tablespoons raw sugar
salt to taste
625ml (1 pt) chicken stock

2 teaspoons dill seed
pepper to taste
yoghurt or cream
ground cinnamon

Boil the pumpkin with the sugar and some salt in barely enough water to cover. When soft, drain off the excess water and push the pumpkin through a sieve, or purée in a blender. Slowly add the chicken stock to the pumpkin purée, stirring well, then add the dill seed. Check the flavour for salt and pepper. Heat through on the stove and, when ready, pour into bowls, putting a spoonful of yoghurt or cream and a dusting of cinnamon on each serving.

DILL-SEED TEA
(1 cup)

Make in the same way as aniseed tea (page 120).

YOGHURT AND DILL CUCUMBERS
(Serves 4)

2 cucumbers
250g (10 oz) yoghurt

1 tablespoon chopped green dill
salt and pepper

Peel the cucumbers thinly, slice them lengthwise, and blanch in salted
water for 5 minutes. Drain well. Mix all the ingredients together in a
shallow dish. Serve chilled, garnished with chopped fresh
or dried dill leaves.

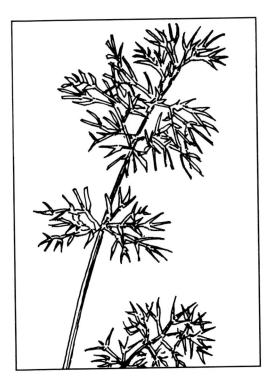

CUCUMBER, PRAWN AND DILL JELLY

(Serves 8 as an appetiser)
(serves 4 as a light luncheon)

This delicate jelly makes an excellent appetiser. In warm weather serve it as a main course for a light luncheon.

2 medium to large cucumbers
250ml (8 fl oz) water
salt to taste
a pinch of pepper
1 tablespoon lemon juice
1 tablespoon gelatine
2 tablespoons hot water

315ml (10 fl oz) cream
green food colouring
150g (6 oz) peeled chopped prawns
1 level tablespoon finely chopped dill leaves
(or 2 teaspoons dried dill)

Peel the cucumbers, cut each in half, scrape out the seeds and chop up roughly. Cook in the water and salt until soft. Take off the stove but do not drain off the liquid. Stir in the pepper, lemon juice, and extra salt if necessary. Press the mixture through a sieve, or purée in a blender. The amount of cucumber purée should be 625ml (1 pt): if not sufficient top up with a little chicken stock. Melt the gelatine in the hot water and stir into the pulp with the cream, a few drops of green colouring, the chopped prawns and dill leaves. Pour into a 1.25 litre (2 pt) mould and place in the refrigerator to set. Serve with sorrel sauce (page 32).

Fennel

Fennel first grew in Mediterranean lands and has been known for so long that it is said to reach as far back as creation. In Greek mythology, Prometheus concealed the fire of the Sun in a hollow fennel stalk and brought it down to Earth from Heaven for the human race. Pliny declares that the herb enables the eye to perceive with clarity the beauty of nature. The belief in fennel's ability to benefit the eyes has persisted through the centuries—it was an old custom to wash the eyes of a newborn baby with fennel water, and herbalists today recommend bathing weakened, sore or inflamed eyes with fennel tea. The use of fennel seed as an aid to digestion is well known, and like aniseed it may be given in small quantities to help young children digest carbohydrates. A weak solution of fennel tea may be given to an uncomfortable baby, with or without milk, to help bring up wind and to soothe the baby. Fennel tea also helps to loosen coughs, and it has a reputation for helping weight-reducers to slim.

As an aid to beauty, a strong, short brew of fennel, cooled, then mixed with a teacup of yoghurt, a little honey and a tablespoon of Fuller's earth, then applied as a face pack, rejuvenates the skin.

A tall plant, 1.2 to 1.5m (4 to 5 ft) high, perennial fennel (*Foeniculum vulgare*) is a familiar sight on waste land and by the roadside when the yellow flowers are in bloom above a froth of greenery. It is often mistakenly referred to as aniseed because the flavour of the leaves and fruit resembles that of anise. However, fennel seed is not as strongly aromatic, is larger, and pale lime-green in colour.

A plant which looks rather like fennel, and is also seen growing wild in open spaces, is Queen Anne's lace, also known as cow parsley and bishop's beard. In reality it is a type of wild carrot which is said to be inedible, but the filmy white flowers look airily decorative when cut for the house.

Another variety of fennel, often called Florence fennel, or finocchio (*F. vulgare dulce*) is a smaller growing annual—75 to 90cm (2½ to 3 ft)—with many uses. The leaves, which are more delicate in flavour than perennial fennel, may be mixed with other greens in a salad, or cooked with fish (a traditional use for leaves of either variety, one reason being that they counteract any oiliness in the fish).

The swollen stem-base of finocchio has a crisp texture and a fragrant aniseed flavour, and is excellent when sliced thinly and tossed in French dressing as a salad, or cut in half and cooked as a vegetable. The seeds can also be used for their health-giving qualities.

Fennel seed may be planted in spring or autumn, but do not sow near caraway or coriander. Fennel also has a harmful effect on dwarf beans, tomatoes and kohlrabi.

Florence fennel, when grown for its bulbous base as a winter vegetable, should be sown in early autumn in a prepared seed-bed with shallow rows. Pick out the seedlings when big enough to handle, and plant them in a sunny position 30 cm (12 in) apart in well-manured ground. As the plants grow, and the base begins to swell, a little earth should be hilled up around each bulge to partly cover it. This procedure is to be continued until the whole bulb is coated as it grows larger. The maturing vegetable must be well watered during this time. When lifting, cut the globe cleanly away from the root system.

If the plants are left to grow without cultivation, the base of the stems will swell only slightly, and their use is more restricted: slice them into salads or trim the greenery away and leave the small bulbs whole for garnishing a cheese board.

The method of collecting seed is identical with that of the other herbs mentioned in this group. The foliage is not usually dried.

Florence fennel cultivated by market gardeners is found in greengrocers' shops during winter and spring. The enormous creamy bulbs are usually tied together by their bushy tops in bundles of two or three. When buying, cut off some of the copious foliage, leaving two or three fronds to store in the cool compartment of the refrigerator for other uses.

FENNEL-SEED TEA

Make in the same way as aniseed tea (page 120).

FENNEL SEED BISCUITS
(About 2 dozen)

100g (4 oz) butter or vegetable
margarine
100g (4 oz) raw sugar
1 beaten egg

2 teaspoons fennel seed
(or 1 teaspoon ground seed)
125g (5 oz) self-raising flour

Cream the butter and sugar, then add the egg, fennel seed and flour.
Pat the mixture thinly on to a greased and floured oven tray, and bake
in a moderate oven (175°C, 350°F) for 45 minutes. Cut into fingers
while hot, cool on the tray and store.

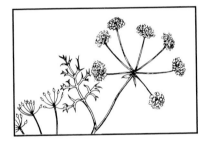

GRILLED FISH WITH FENNEL

For each person, 1 whole
cleaned fish
salt and freshly ground pepper

slices of lemon, cut very thin
1 small bunch green fennel

Remove the head from each fish, then wash and place on a board.
With a sharp knife make about 4 incisions on one side across the fish
(from edge to edge). Dust the uncut side with salt and pepper, and
place under the griller with the cut side down. When the uncut side is
cooked, turn the fish over carefully and press lemon pieces into
alternate incisions, then press 2-inch-long fennel fronds into the
remaining incisions. Season with salt and pepper, place under the
griller again and cook until done.
If the fish seems dry during cooking, brush vegetable oil
over both sides.

FENNEL OR FINOCCHIO SALAD
(Serves 2)

Take one large fennel bulb and trim off the stalks, then wash the globe thoroughly under running water. With a sharp knife, slice it thinly across, separating the circles like onion rings. Pat dry, and place in a wooden bowl with salt, freshly ground pepper, 2 tablespoons vegetable oil and 1 tablespoon white or cider vinegar. Toss well and serve. For a change, add a few torn-up lettuce leaves to the fennel salad, with some pitted black olives and chopped parsley.

FENNEL BULBS WITH WHITE SAUCE
(Serves 4)

To serve as a vegetable, or to eat as a light luncheon dish.

2 fennel bulbs	2 tablespoons grated
1 cup thick white sauce	tasty cheese

Trim the bulbs, wash them and cut each one in half lengthwise. Drop them into boiling water and simmer for 20 minutes. Drain, then lay the cut side down in an ovenproof dish. Mask with sauce (recipe below) and sprinkle with cheese, then place under the griller or put in a hot oven (210°C, 400°F) for a few minutes, until the cheese melts and browns a little.

White sauce: Melt 1 tablespoon butter or margarine in a saucepan over medium heat. Stir in 2 tablespoons unbleached flour, add 250ml (8 fl oz) milk and stir until thick.

Winter

**A WARMING FAMILY OF
PUNGENT HERBS**
*hyssop marjoram oregano
rosemary sage savory thyme*

**A COLLECTION OF RESTORATIVE
AND TONIC HERBS**
*chicory comfrey garlic
horseradish horehound*

I love snow, and all the forms
of the radiant frost:
I love waves, and winds, and storms,
Everything almost
Which is Nature's, and may be
Untainted by man's misery.

PERCY BYSSHE SHELLEY   Song, v. 6.

With the onset of winter, and the slowing down of much plant growth, work in the garden goes at a more leisurely pace. This dormant cycle of the year brings opportunities for tidying up, and it is also a good time for other odd jobs overlooked in the bustle of gathering autumn's harvest.

This is the time when jars of the different seasons' yield from the preserving pan are opened and savoured. It is the time, too—when all is cold and dreary outside—to take lids off bottles and inhale the scents of summer in the concentrated fragrance of dried herbs . . . to stir pot-pourri and feel the fragile smoothness of paper-thin rose-petals, and the brittle fabric of pungent geranium-leaves, while the soft aroma drifts upward . . . to see that clove pomanders are hanging in closets to keep clothes fresh and free from hibernating insects . . . and to unfold chilly sheets, smelling sweetly and sunnily of verbena and lavender that have been dried in the linen cupboard.

If you haven't the time, or the garden, to be able to gather, dry and preserve, most of the dried herbs and teas are available in grocery shops and delicatessens these days, while pot-pourri and lavender articles are found in gift shops or in shops specialising in handcrafted articles.

Among the herbs of particular interest now are certain members of the extremely redolent Labiatae family, namely hyssop, marjoram, oregano, rosemary, sage, savory and thyme. If you look at the lipped flowers of any of the members of this family, beloved by bees, you will see that they are identical in form, whether small or large.

These plants possess vital life-giving forces in their every part: root, stalk, leaves and flowers are permeated with a cheering vigour that helps to drive away chills while warming and harmonizing the system—qualities especially welcome during colder weather. Although these sturdy perennials grow throughout summer and

Herbs for all seasons

have many uses in hot-weather cooking, one of their particular virtues is in their ability, whether fresh or dried, to enliven heavier food: their aromatic spiciness combines well with robust dishes, and their nutritional contribution is high.

This family with its leaves growing from hard, five-angled stems, drinks in the sunlight and turns it into rich, volatile oils and valuable mineral substances. It has been said that these plants have much in common with salt, yet in a living form, and their use has been recommended for a substitute flavour in salt-free diets.

The position they like best when growing is in full sun, and the soil must be well-drained; they do very well in rockeries.

For drying, full flavour is retained if stalks are picked just as the plants are coming into flower in late summer or autumn, and in the morning after the dew has evaporated from the leaves. Tie the herbs in bundles and hang in the shade, or lay the branches on airy racks. When quite dry, crumble the leaves from the stems and store in airtight containers, or pack the whole dried stalks with leaves still on them into boxes or jars and close tightly.

There are two perennial herbs belonging to the Labiatae family which are not used in cooking, but they are interesting plants, well worth having in the garden. One is cat-thyme or cat-sage (*Teucrium marum*), the other is catnip (*Nepeta cataria*). Shrubby cat-thyme's lipped, rosy, flowers sparkle amongst the stiff grey leaves in summer and autumn. Pick a sprig and notice how piercingly its ether-scent tingles in the nostrils. Grow catnip or, as it is sometimes called, catmint, for your cat. (Do not confuse it with another type of catmint, *N. mussini*, which is low-growing and has grey leaves and mauve flowers: it is pretty, but not the true catnip beloved by the feline race.) Catnip is not an attractive plant: it grows tall and lanky and rather untidily, with soft, hoary-green leaves and autumn-blooming heads of pallid, whitish flowerets. Don't plant it in a conspicuous place, but tuck it into a corner where your cat may roll in it.

The restorative and tonic herbs in this chapter are chicory, comfrey, garlic, horseradish and horehound. Most are excellent herbs for cold weather cooking, and all may be used in simple remedies for winter ills. They do not belong to one family but represent several plant clans. There is not one method for growing, propagating, harvesting and drying them all, so each one's requirements are described as we go along.

Hyssop

Hyssop (*Hyssopus officinalis*) is not as widely known as many herbs used today. A native of southern Europe, it belongs to the Labiatae family.

The history of the herb is controversial: some say it is the hyssop of the Bible—it grows wild in the Holy Land, and so do thyme, marjoram, mint, rosemary and lavender. Some authorities have said the hyssop of Scripture is one of the wild marjorams. Two eminent scholars disagree, and identify Holy Hyssop with the caper plant (*Capparis spinosa*), which grows in the valleys of Kedron and the Jordan. This plant seeds itself on the walls of old temples and ancient ruins.

There are several kinds of hyssop, with flowers of pink, white or deep blue which bloom during summer and early autumn. A dwarf species, *H. aristatus*, is a compact rock plant with an even longer flowering period.

While it is not certain whether the hyssop we know is the biblical herb, its wonderful healing powers are undisputed. Old herbalists and physicians praised its effectiveness in curing many illnesses. The green tops are brewed as a tea to improve the tone of a weak stomach, and are boiled in a soup which has been given for asthma. An infusion of the leaves, sometimes also mixed with horehound and taken frequently as an expectorant, relieves catarrh. A tea made from the dried flowers of hyssop is an old remedy for weakness of the chest. For external application, an infusion of the leaves has been employed for muscular rheumatism, for bruises and for discoloured contusions. The green herb, bruised and applied, has been known to heal cuts. Edmund Spenser remarks on this: 'Sharp hishop, good for greens woundes remedies.' Tusser included hyssop in his list of herbs for strewing in chambers.

A fine, ethereal oil distilled from the leaves, stems and flowers is valued more highly than oil of lavender by perfumers. Oil of hyssop was often employed in the making of liqueurs, Chartreuse among them. Honey from hyssop flowers is said to be particularly delicate and fragrant.

The hyssop we have in the garden has tufts of tiny lipped flowers of a vibrant cobalt-blue, and grows between 18 and 24 inches high. In appearance the shrubby plant looks very like winter savory, except for the colour of the blooms. It is an evergreen perennial, with the same type of narrow green leaves as winter savory, and they have an aromatic, peppery taste reminiscent of that of savory, only more subtly piquant. In cooking, hyssop may be interchanged with savory. Try the chopped leaves with all kinds of beans and with other vegetables; in soups, sauces and salads; with meat, fish and poultry; and mixed into cottage cheese.

Hyssop seed may be sown in spring or autumn, roots may be divided in spring or autumn, and propagation by cuttings is carried out in spring. Plants like to grow in light, well-drained soil in part sun. As they can grow over 60cm (2 ft) high and become very bushy, they should be kept 30 to 60cm (12 to 24 in) apart. They have been used in old gardens as low hedges for mazes, and are still valued for borders. For drying, follow the method on page 127. The dried flowers are used in teas, so if wishing to dry them yourself for this purpose, wait until the plant is in full bloom before harvesting. When the stalks, leaves and flowers are brittle, strip off the flowers into separate containers.

In companion planting, hyssop planted near grapevines is said to increase the yield of grapes. It inhibits the growth of radishes. Hyssop attracts the cabbage butterfly away from cabbages. Blue hyssop is an insect repellent. Honey-bees are especially attracted to hyssop flowers.

QUICK PROTEIN LUNCH FLAVOURED WITH HYSSOP

1 x 300g (12 oz) can tuna	1 teaspoon chopped hyssop
50g (2 oz) cottage cheese	leaves
1 egg yolk	salt and pepper

Drain the can of tuna and mash the fish with the cottage cheese, egg yolk and hyssop leaves, adding salt and pepper to taste.

HYSSOP TEA

An old recipe for weakness of the chest. Pour a pint of cool water over 5g (¼ oz) dried hyssop flowers. Cover and steep overnight. Strain and sweeten with honey, and take a wineglassful three times a day.

HONEYED CARROT STRAWS WITH HYSSOP
(Serves 3 or 4)

2 medium carrots
1 tablespoon water
1 teaspoon honey

2 teaspoons finely chopped hyssop
salt and pepper

Cut the carrots into straws and place in a saucepan with the rest of the ingredients. Cover and simmer slowly for 10 minutes. Serve hot.

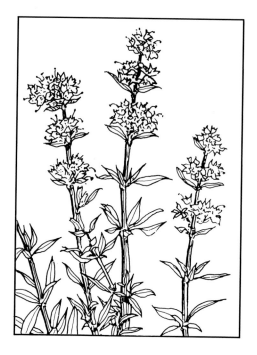

Herbs for all seasons

YORKSHIRE PUDDING WITH HYSSOP
OR SAVORY

3 tablespoons vegetable oil
25g (3 oz) self-raising flour
salt to taste

1 large egg
150ml (5 fl oz) milk
1 teaspoon finely chopped hyssop

Heat the oil in an oblong tin in a 175°C or 350°F oven. Sift the flour and salt into a bowl, then stir in the egg, milk and hyssop. When the oil is smoking hot, pour the batter in and bake for 15 to 20 minutes. Serve hot, cut into squares, with roast beef.

RAW CAULIFLOWER AND HYSSOP SALAD
(Serves 6)

1 small cauliflower, or ½ larger
cauliflower
1 apple, chopped into
small dice with peel
left on

2 tablespoons finely chopped
hyssop
2 teaspoons salt
250g (10 oz) yoghurt
1 tablespoon lemon juice

Trim and wash the cauliflower. Slice the flowers and the tender portions of the stalks paper-thin, and mix with the chopped apple in a bowl. Add the hyssop, salt, yoghurt and lemon juice, toss well together and chill. The salad may be decorated with hyssop sprigs.

Marjoram and Oregano

Marjoram (*Origanum majorana.*) and oregano (*O. vulgare*) are together here because of their close relationship, oregano being a wild form of marjoram. They belong to the Labiatae family and are perennials.

Marjoram's native habitat is Asia, Europe and North Africa. People's knowledge of it goes back to the days of mythology which says that Venus was the first to raise marjoram, taking it from the waters of the vast ocean to the top of the highest mountain where it was closest to the sun's dynamic rays. Its generic name, *Origanum*, means 'joy of the mountains'. In Egypt it was dedicated to the Sun-God Osiris, and it was offered on the altars of Greek and Roman temples.

Greek physicians used marjoram or oregano extensively, both internally and externally. The warmth forces it has accumulated from the sun helps put right bad colds, cramps and digestive disorders. Hot fomentations of the dried leaves and tops applied in bags is helpful to painful swellings, rheumatism and colic. An infusion of the leaves taken as a tea relieves nervous headaches, induces sleep, stimulates excretion and is recommended as a spring tea.

For growing in the garden there are several kinds of marjoram. Knotted marjoram, with softly fragrant greyish leaves, is a perennial in warm climates but, being tender, dies away in severe winters. The flowers appear in autumn in small pearly tufts sprouting from tight green 'knots'. The more hardy, bushy marjoram, with leaves just as sweet and fragrant, has tiny white autumn-bearing flowers shooting from green bracts. It grows to 60cm (2 ft) high. Oregano flowers open at the same time as those of marjoram and are identical to this type, but the plant is more sprawling in habit; it grows to about 45cm (18 in) and the leaves are coarser, greener and more pungent. It is a very popular herb in Italian cooking. The Greeks call it rigani, and in both Greek and Italian cooking it is the dried flower tops which are mainly used.

There is another marjoram, a small kind sometimes grown as an indoor plant, known as Dittany of Crete (*O. dictamnus*). It was formerly a favourite with country cottagers, who called it hop plant because of its flowers, which look like miniature pink hops. By the way, the names Margaret and Marjorie, meaning 'pearl', are derived from marjoram.

All marjorams thrive in light, well-drained soil in full sun, but with shelter from cold winds. Sow seed in spring or autumn, or propagate from cuttings or root divisions taken in spring. Plant several bushes of the same species about 30cm (12in) apart from one another. They are attractive for borders and rockeries, and have a beneficial effect on surrounding plants.

Harvest marjoram and oregano for drying as described on page 126.

As marjoram, thyme and sage comprise the traditional mixed herbs, try making your own blend for winter use when the dried leaves are ready. A suggested mixture is one part each of marjoram and thyme to two parts of sage. The reason for having a double quantity of sage is that thyme and marjoram when dried are so forceful that if an equal amount is used they would overpower the drier flavour of sage. For a special bouquet, also add one part of parsley and an even smaller amount of mint.

Try marjoram either fresh or dried on its own in many dishes. (I like it as much as basil and use it in the same way—marjoram leaves have a softer balminess, with more depth.) Sprinkle marjoram on salads, mix it into omelettes, sauces, scones and dumplings, use it with fish and poultry dishes, in clear soups, and with cooked, buttered vegetables.

The flavour of dried oregano is immensely strong and penetrating, especially if the plant has started flowering when harvested. It dries more quickly than any herb I know, possibly because of the high concentration of aromatic, volatile oils in the leaves, flowers and stems, and the minimum of watery material. This zesty herb goes into hearty dishes: it is used with pasta and rice, in pizzas, moussaka, tomato dishes and meat loaf, and is sprinkled on lamb and pork before grilling or roasting.

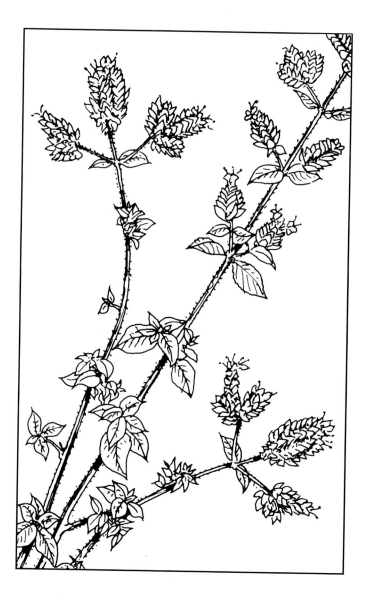

MARJORAM JELLY

Wash a big bunch of marjoram—about 50 stalks. Place in a saucepan
with enough water to cover, add the peel from a lemon, and simmer
for 1 hour. Strain the liquid into a bowl and add the juice of 3 lemons.
Measure, allowing ½ cup sugar to every cup of liquid. Return the
marjoram syrup to the saucepan and bring slowly to the boil. Drop in
a little green colouring. Add fruit pectin, which is available from
health food shops (directions for the correct proportions will be on
the packet). Stir, take off the stove, skim off any foam, and seal into
clean dry jars. Use as an accompaniment to main course dishes, and
as a delicious spread for buttered hot scones.

WHOLEWHEAT HERB SCONES
(About 2 dozen)

*Mixed herbs are indispensable in the breadcrumb seasonings for baked
poultry, meats and fish, as well as for flavouring rissoles and meat loaf. A
lesser known use for them is in scones, which we have found delicious.*

185g (7½ oz) wholewheat flour	50g (2 oz) butter or margarine
1 teaspoon baking powder	1 teaspoon mixed herbs
1 pinch salt	4-5 tablespoons natural yoghurt
1 teaspoon raw sugar	

Sift the dry ingredients, flour, baking powder, salt and sugar into a
bowl. Rub in the butter until the mixture resembles breadcrumbs, then
stir in the herbs. Using a knife, bind the mixture with the yoghurt to
form a soft dough. Pat out on a floury surface to form a square, then,
with a sharp knife, mark the scones into sections. Lift on to a buttered
and floured baking tray and bake in a hot oven (210°C, 400°F) for
20 to 25 minutes. Split the scones and eat them hot or
cold with butter.

Marjoram and Oregano

MARJORAM TEA
(1 cup)

With dried leaves: Pour 250ml (8 fl oz) boiling water over 1 teaspoon marjoram leaves, cover and infuse for several minutes. Strain, sweeten with honey if wished.
With fresh leaves: Using 1 tablespoon coarsely chopped marjoram leaves make tea in the same way as above. Take for nervous headaches, indigestion and bad breath, and for morning sickness in early pregnancy.

STEAK AND KIDNEY CASSEROLE WITH WHOLEWHEAT OREGANO DUMPLINGS
(Serves 3 or 4)

400g (1 lb) steak and kidney, chopped and mixed together
3 rounded tablespoons wholewheat flour
2 large cloves garlic, chopped
1 small onion, chopped
2 medium carrots, coarsely chopped
1 outside stalk celery, coarsely chopped

salt to taste
½ teaspoon each dried thyme and marjoram (or 1 spray each fresh thyme and marjoram)
1 teaspoon dried sage (or 2 sprays fresh sage)
315ml (10 fl oz) water or stock

Roll the meat in the flour and toss into an ovenproof casserole dish with the rest of the ingredients, pouring the water in last. Put the lid on and place in a 150°C or 300°F oven for 1½ to 2 hours (stir once or twice during this time). During the last 20 minutes of cooking, remove the twigs if using fresh herbs—the leaves will have floated off into the gravy. Then drop the dumplings on top of the bubbling gravy in the casserole, replace the lid and continue cooking for the remaining 20 minutes.

Wholewheat oregano dumplings
Sift together 125g (5 oz) wholewheat flour, 1½ teaspoons baking powder and a pinch of salt. Rub in 2 tablespoons butter or margarine until the mixture is the texture of breadcrumbs. With a knife, stir in 1 tablespoon chopped fresh oregano (or 2 teaspoons

dried oregano) and 2 tablespoons plain yoghurt. With floured hands roll the dough into balls and drop them into the casserole dish to cook as described above.

STEAMED MARJORAM CHICKEN
(Serves 2 or 3)

1 x 800g (2 lb) chicken
315ml (10 fl oz) water
juice of ½ lemon
salt to taste

pinch of pepper
3 sprays fresh marjoram (or 2
teaspoons dried marjoram)

Place the chicken on a strong saucer in a saucepan. Add the water, then sprinkle the lemon juice over the chicken, followed by the salt and pepper. Lay the marjoram over the bird's breast and put the lid tightly on the saucepan. Bring the water to the boil, then turn the heat down and simmer slowly for 2 hours.
If eating the chicken hot, remove it to a serving dish and keep it hot while you thicken the stock with 1 tablespoon cornstarch blended to a smooth paste with a little milk. Pour this sauce all over the chicken and serve.
If eating the chicken cold, put the bird in a deep bowl or dish and pour stock over it without thickening. Cool, then cover and place in the refrigerator overnight. Next day, the juice will have jellied, but the thin film of fat that will have formed must be skimmed off. The chicken will be tender and succulent.

HERBED MEAT LOAF

(serves 4)

600g (1½ lb) ground round
100g (4 oz) soft wholewheat
breadcrumbs
1 green pepper, finely chopped
1 onion, finely chopped
½ teaspoon soy sauce
1 teaspoon French mustard

salt to taste
½ teaspoon dried thyme
½ teaspoon marjoram
1 teaspoon dried sage
2 eggs, beaten
3 tablespoons vegetable oil

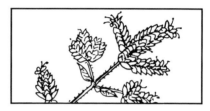

Mash together in a bowl, using a fork, all the ingredients except the
last two. Bind the mixture with the beaten eggs, then pack the mince
into a loaf tin which has been moistened with a little oil. Place in the
refrigerator for at least 1 hour. Turn the loaf into a baking dish (it
will come out easily) and pour the oil over it. Bake in a 175°C or
350°F oven for 1 hour. Serve hot with either of the following sauces.

Tomato sauce

Stew 400g (1 lb) peeled tomatoes and 1 tablespoon chopped
marjoram with a little water; or empty one 375g (15 oz) can of
tomatoes with their liquid into a saucepan and heat with the
marjoram, seasoning to taste with salt and pepper or a pinch of
cayenne. Thicken with a good tablespoon of cornstarch blended with
a little milk. Serve in a sauce boat to accompany the meat loaf,
or pour the sauce over the loaf and serve.

Mushroom sauce

Wash, peel and slice thinly 200g (8 oz) mushrooms. Fry them lightly
in a pan in a tablespoon of melted butter or margarine. Pour 250ml
(8 fl oz) stock into the pan and flavour with salt, pepper and a
generous pinch of ground nutmeg. When the liquid is simmering,
thicken with a good tablespoon of cornstarch blended with a little
milk. Serve in a sauce boat with the meat loaf or pour the sauce over
the loaf before serving.

ZUCCHINI OREGANO SALAD

(Serves 6)

800g (2 lb) small zucchini
4 tablespoons chopped shallots
1 sweet red pepper, chopped
2 tablespoons chopped parsley
1 tablespoon chopped oregano
120ml (4 oz) vegetable oil

3 tablespoons cider vinegar
salt to taste
freshly ground pepper
2 teaspoons honey
200g (8 oz) black olives, pitted

Slice the ends off and cut the zucchini into circles. Drop them into boiling, salted water, cook for 2 minutes, then drain well in a colander. When cool, transfer the zucchini to a bowl and add the red pepper, parsley and oregano. Put the oil, vinegar, salt, pepper and honey into a screw-top glass jar, shake well and pour over the zucchini. Toss and chill. To serve, line a large flat glass platter, or a wooden salad bowl, with crisp lettuce leaves or a selection of green herb leaves, and pile the zucchini on to them.
Strew the top with olives.

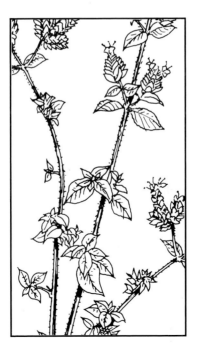

MOUSSAKA
(Serves 4)

*Oregano spikes this nourishing, tasty Greek dish, or at least the version
which my son Dick and his wife Elizabeth tasted during their travels not
long after they were married. After a day spent in the ruins of Olympia, and
a good night's sleep in a nearby village, as the sun rose over the stones of
Zeus's temple they set their faces to Mycenae. After several hours' driving in
clear autumn weather through ancient Arcadia and a landscape of pines
and craggy villages, they arrived ravenously hungry at a taverna from which
savoury smells were emanating. As is customary, they went into the kitchen
and pointed to whichever dish appealed: moussaka was their choice, served
piping hot in the shells. This is Elizabeth's recipe.*

<table>
<tr><td>2 large eggplants</td><td>2 tablespoons tomato paste</td></tr>
<tr><td>4 tablespoons olive oil</td><td>2 tablespoons chopped fresh</td></tr>
<tr><td>1 onion, chopped</td><td>oregano (or 1 tablespoon dried</td></tr>
<tr><td>2 cloves garlic, chopped</td><td>oregano)</td></tr>
<tr><td>600g (1½ lb) ground lamb or</td><td>salt to taste</td></tr>
<tr><td>sirloin</td><td>Parmesan cheese, grated</td></tr>
<tr><td>400g (1 lb) tomatoes, peeled and</td><td></td></tr>
<tr><td>cut up</td><td></td></tr>
</table>

Wash and halve the eggplants. Heat the oil in a heavy frying-pan and
fry the eggplant for 5 minutes on each side. Drain on absorbent
paper. Place the onion and garlic in the pan to soften, then stir in the
meat, tomatoes, tomato paste, oregano and salt. Scoop the centres
carefully from the eggplants, then chop up and mix it into the other
ingredients. Cook slowly until the mixture is amalgamated and
mushy. (If it is a little dry, add some red wine.) Place the eggplant
shells in an ovenproof dish and pack some mixture into each one.
Sprinkle the tops with a generous amount of Parmesan and bake in a
moderate oven (175°C, 350°F) until the cheese melts. Serve hot.

Rosemary

Cloaked in mystical legends, rosemary (*Rosmarinus officinalis*), of the Labiatae family, is a powerful herb filled with potent forces.

Who has not heard the saying that rosemary is for remembrance? These words come down from the earliest times, for it has long been known that rosemary helps all the functions of the head, relieving nervous headaches, promoting a healthy scalp and hair, and assisting the memory. In ancient Greece, students studying for their examinations threaded sprigs of rosemary in their locks to encourage clear thinking and a good memory. Shakespeare was familiar with herbs and their qualities:

> OPHELIA: *There's rosemary, that's for remembrance;*
> *pray love, remember.*
>
> Hamlet, 4, V.

Break off a piece of rosemary, crush the green, needle-like leaves in your fingers, and inhale the bracing perfume while keeping your eyes closed. The mind becomes crystal-clear as the plant's penetrating vapour seems to course through the brain cells, giving each cell a stirring tingle.

Shampoos and hair lotions containing pure extract of rosemary will bring new life to scalp and hair while preventing dandruff. Our family and many friends have used a rosemary shampoo for several years with dramatic improvement in hair health. A simple home-made lotion of leafy rosemary branches simmered in water for 30 minutes, strained and cooled, then poured over the hair as a final rinse, may be used by anyone who has a rosemary bush.

Another of rosemary's virtues is its aid to digestion, especially of starchy foods and rich meats like pork and veal. It is also a piquant relish for beef and lamb, and many vegetables—eggplant, zucchini and lima beans particularly.

Its stimulating qualities are excellent in body lotions and bath essences, and when used in the morning help to give an alertness for the day ahead. I have used a fresh resin-scented rosemary bath milk for a morning bath, and found it invigorating. Oil of rosemary is one of the ingredients in genuine eau-de-Cologne, which makes a refreshing rub in hot, tiring weather. Hungary Water, famous for centuries, was invented, according to tradition, by a hermit for a Queen of Hungary who suffered from paralysed limbs: its continual application is said to have cured her. Eleanour Sinclair Rohde writes that this recipe is still preserved in the Imperial Library of Vienna.

Rosemary wine is a quietening cordial for the nerves, and is stimulating for the kidneys.

Rosemary tea taken warm helps sufferers from headaches, colic and colds, and is said to relieve nervous depression.

Of the many legends about rosemary, there is a popular one telling how a rosemary bush will never grow taller than the height of Christ (1.5 to 1.8 m or 5 to 6 ft) when He was a man on earth, and that after 33 years the plant increases in breadth, but not in height.

Another holy story says that during the flight into Egypt the Virgin Mary threw her robe over a rosemary bush while she rested beside it. For ever afterwards the flowers, which had been white, turned the blue colour of her garment.

Some stories tell how rosemary was used to try to awaken Sleeping Beauty.

The Sicilians tell their children that young fairies taking the form of snakes lie amongst the branches of rosemary bushes.

It is believed that rosemary grew in England before the Norman Conquest, and that it was possibly brought to Britain by the early Romans from its native Mediterranean rocky shores. However, it had a lapse in popularity for some years until it was reintroduced by Philippa, wife to Edward III. A famous manuscript dealing with the virtues of rosemary, sent by Queen Philippa's mother, the Countess of Hainault, is preserved in the library of Trinity College, Cambridge.

There are several kinds of rosemary, the two most widely grown being the bushy, upright type (*R. officinalis*) and a decorative, horizontal type (*R. prostratus*) which usually grows no more than 30 cm (12 in) high. They both like well-drained, sandy soil and a sunny position. True to its name, *Rosmarinus*, meaning 'dew of the sea', rosemary grows most vigorously on the coast, where the saline essence of the plant seems more pronounced. We recently saw a bush of prostrate rosemary growing by the sea, and it had reached a height of nearly 90 cm (3 ft), while its branches twisted and spread octopus-fashion over the stones nearby. Both kinds have mist-blue flowers which are in bloom during winter and spring.

Propagation is by sowing seed in spring or autumn, or by semi-hardwood cuttings taken with a heel in spring. Prostrate rosemary is ideal for rockeries, and the upright form is happy with a sheltering wall behind it. A rewarding and hardy evergreen perennial, upright rosemary is also suitable for hedge-work and, like rue, keeps 'seeming and savour all the winter long' (Shakespeare, *The Winter's Tale*, 4, III).

In companion planting, rosemary and sage grow well together, besides showing one another to advantage with contrasting foliage of spiky iridescent green and soft, opalescent grey.

To dry rosemary follow the method given on page 126.

ROSEMARY WINE

For a beneficial tonic for the nerves and kidneys chop up sprigs of fresh rosemary to make 1 tablespoon, then pour 500ml (16 fl oz) white wine over the leaves. Cover and infuse for 2 days. Strain, and sip a small quantity at a time.

EGGPLANT AND ROSEMARY CASSEROLE
(Serves 4 to 6)

1 medium to large eggplant, sliced thinly with peel left on
2 medium tomatoes, sliced thinly
1 onion, peeled and chopped
4 cloves garlic, chopped
2 teaspoons finely chopped fresh rosemary (or 1 teaspoon crumbled dried rosemary)
1 tablespoon chopped parsley
1 tablespoon vegetable oil
salt and freshly ground pepper

Place half of each of the above ingredients in layers in a casserole dish. Repeat the layers with the rest of the ingredients in the same way. Put the lid on and bake in a medium oven (150–160°C, 300–325°F) for 1 hour. Serve hot.

GREEN LIMA BEAN AND ROSEMARY SALAD
(Serves 4)

300g (12 oz) frozen or canned small lima beans
1 tablespoon finely chopped fresh rosemary (or 2 teaspoons crumbled dried rosemary)
2 shallots, finely chopped

1 clove garlic, finely chopped
1 can anchovy fillets, drained and coarsely chopped
4 tablespoons vegetable oil
1 tablespoon white vinegar or lemon juice

Boil the frozen beans in salted water until cooked, about 10 minutes, or open the can of lima beans. Drain, turn into a bowl and add rosemary, shallots, garlic and anchovies. Mix the oil and vinegar together, pour over the salad and toss well.

HERBED DRUMSTICKS
(Serves 2 or 3)

Put 6 chicken drumsticks in a baking dish, and dust with salt and freshly ground pepper. Pour over them 1 tablespoon vegetable oil, and dot with butter or margarine. Finish with 2 teaspoons finely chopped rosemary, 1 teaspoon chopped marjoram, and 1 thick slice of bacon coarsely chopped. Bake uncovered in a medium oven (175°C, 350°F) for 1 hour. To serve, arrange the drumsticks on a plate and keep hot. Drain the baking dish of the fat except for 1 tablespoon and any 'bits', then blend in 1 heaped teaspoon flour. Stir in 125ml (4 fl oz) stock. When the gravy has thickened pour into a small jug and serve with the drumsticks.

ROSEMARY TEA
(1 cup)

As a remedy for headache, colic and colds take 2 or 3 tops of rosemary, either flowering or not, and place in a small teapot, then pour 250ml (8 fl oz) boiling water over them. Cover and infuse for several minutes, then strain and drink warm. The tea may be sweetened with honey if wished.

Sage

Sage, or *Salvia*, belonging to the Labiatae family, originated in Mediterranean lands and was brought by the Romans wherever they went to settle. It has long had the reputation of retarding old age, of restoring energy and failing memory, and of aiding the digestion. It also brings colour back to greying hair when included in hair tonics. Sage is known for its healing properties for throat and mouth: there are many gargles and mouth-washes that include it as the principal ingredient. The leaves rubbed across the teeth regularly help to whiten them and will strengthen the gums too. Leafy sprigs of sage were among the strewing herbs spread with rushes on the floors of old manors, which was done because sage was believed to be an antiseptic against plague and other infections. There is good reason for the choice of its botanical name, *Salvia*, meaning health.

In cooking, sage helps to counteract the richness in foods such as pork, goose, duck and oily fish; it also combines well with dairy foods and with bean and pea soups. Sage makes a pleasing, beneficial tea. With thyme and marjoram, it traditionally goes into mixed herbs.

There are several kinds of sage. The purple-flowered *S. officinalis* is the one most commonly used in cooking and it has excellent healing properties, although red sage is said to be the most effective medicinally. With its leaves of a maroon colour, red sage is not to be confused with the red-flowering salvia seen frequently in park plantings.

Shrubby sage plants grow up to 90cm (3 ft) high with square and woody stems. The pewter-grey leaves are honeycombed with minute veins, giving them a grainy feel, and their scent and flavour is as aromatic as that of lavender, without the sweetness and with their own curious, dry pungency. The plant blooms in autumn, and often in spring too. Bees love the nectar-filled heliotrope-coloured flowers. Sir John Hill, MD, an eighteenth-century author of herbals, says that there are certain juice contained in particular parts of plants at certain seasons:

Just when the flowers of sage begin to open there is in their cups a fragrant resin of this kind, highly flavoured, balmy, delicate, and to the taste one of the most delicious cordials that can be thought, warm and aromatic. I no longer doubted anything that had been said of sage; the smell, the taste, the flavour here promised all.

Sage seed may be sown in spring and autumn, or propagated by cuttings and root division in spring. Plants need well-drained soil—if possible on the limy and gravelly side. They do best with a sheltering wall behind them. If drying the leaves for winter use, follow the directions for drying described on page 126. Sage is a perennial plant, and should be cut back hard after flowering.

In companion planting, sage and rosemary aid one another. Sage also helps to repel cabbage butterfly, and is said to improve the flavour and digestibility of cabbages if grown amongst them.

SAGE TEA
(1 cup)

Takes as a general health tea, for stress, and for shock.
With dried leaves Pour 250ml (8 fl oz) boiling water over 1 teaspoon sage leaves, cover and infuse for several minutes. Strain, and sweeten with honey if wished.
With fresh leaves Use 1 tablespoon coarsely chopped sage leaves and make in the same way as above.

MIXTURE FOR A SORE THROAT OR COUGH

Pour a pint of boiling water on a handful of sage leaves, and when moderately cool add a little vinegar and honey. Take a teaspoonful at a time; use also as a gargle.

ELEANOUR SINCLAIR ROHDE A Garden of Herbs

SAGE AND MILK GARGLE AND MOUTHWASH

This recipe was given to me by a new German arrival. Put 250ml (8 fl oz) milk into a saucepan and add 2 teaspoons dried sage, or 1 heaped tablespoon chopped fresh sage. Bring slowly to simmering point, cover and cool. Strain and use as a gargle or mouthwash.

MIXED HERB AND BREADCRUMB SEASONING

100g (4 oz) soft wholewheat breadcrumbs
1 tablespoon finely chopped white onion
1 teaspoon dried sage
½ teaspoon dried thyme
½ teaspoon dried marjoram
a pinch of salt and pepper
a squeeze of lemon juice
10 g (½ oz) butter or margarine, cut into small pieces

Mix all the ingredients well together and use to stuff poultry or boned meat. For a more binding texture, the yolk of an egg may be added but if you like a lighter type of seasoning add a little milk instead. An unusual tang is imparted to the seasoning if you add a pinch of curry powder, blending it in well.

A TONIC AND RESTORATIVE FOR THE HAIR

An old recipe from *Lotions and Potions*.
Infuse in vinegar: rosemary, sage, southernwood; allow to stand in bottle in a sunny window for seven to eight days before straining.

SAGE-FLAVOURED LAMB

Prepare a leg of lamb several hours before cooking. Make several incisions across the top, then press a little finely chopped garlic and crumbled dried sage, or chopped fresh sage, into each slit. Place the leg in a baking dish, pour 125ml (4 fl oz) of red wine over it, sprinkle with herb or vegetable salt, and leave for at least 5 hours before putting it into a hot oven (210°C, 400°F) to bake. After 30 minutes, spoon the liquor in the dish over the meat, and add 125ml (4 fl oz) vegetable oil. Continue baking until the leg is cooked, basting occasionally. Vegetables may be placed around the joint in the usual way. The gravy made from the pan juices is dark brown and very tasty.

Savory

There are several kinds of savory and all have a distinguishing peppery taste. In Germany one of this herb's everyday names is pepper herb. Savories embody, to a marked degree, the warm elements of the Labiatae family, whose members are especially notable for their pungency.

The savories are native to the Mediterranean region and were introduced to Britain by the Romans. Later they were among the first herbs taken to the New World by the Pilgrim Fathers. The two kinds most popular today are perennial winter savory (*Satureia montana*) and annual summer savory (*S. hortensis*). The name of the genus has been linked with the satyrs of mythology, and there is evidence that the savories were cultivated in remote ages. Their medicinal properties were valued for the treatment of colic, flatulence, giddiness and respiratory troubles. Culpeper wrote that savory is good for 'affections of the breast', and that 'it expels tough phelgm from the chest and lungs'. In cooking, use this herb to help digest many foods, especially leguminous vegetables such as all members of the bean family. (Savory is often known in Germany as *bohnen-kraut*, and in Holland as *boonen kruid*, both meaning bean herb.)

Winter savory is a shrubby plant, growing to a height of 45cm (18 in). It has woody stalks and narrow, firm leaves of shiny green. The diminutive plumes of snow-white flowers appear in summer and autumn. There is a lesser known form of winter savory. *S. montana* var. *subspicata*, whose leaves are a little smaller and lusher, and the white flowers are more thickly clustered than those of upright savory: it spreads in dense cushiony mounds, making a very attractive plant for borders, or for filling pockets in rustic paved paths and terraces, and in dry stone walls. Cut back this prostrate variety hard when the cold weather starts, and it will reward you by flourishing even more the following summer. Propagation is by root division or cuttings taken in spring—this particular form cannot be relied on to be true to type from seed. For upright winter savory, sow seed in spring or autumn, or propagate by root division or cuttings in spring.

Summer savory grows up to 60 cm (2 ft) tall, with slender bronze-green leaves, and pale pink flowers in summer and autumn. When the seed is sown early in spring the plant is ready to pick at the beginning of summer. It is a good idea to have successive sowings into the middle of summer, and then to begin harvesting the final crop in late autumn.

All savories like to grow in well-drained, light soil in a sunny position. In companion planting, summer savory as a border helps both onions and green beans. Winter savory is an insect repellent.

For drying, follow the method given on page 126.

When picking winter savory fresh, I find several inches of the tender tops are the most satisfactory to use. In winter, the plant reduces to a much lower shrub, and the leaves become quite unyielding, so if using them green, chop them very finely. When it is dried, crumble winter savory as small as you can, but if it is very hard grind it in a blender. Both fresh and dried summer savory leaves are softer.

The peppery relish of savories not only gives beans a lift, but the herb may be mixed with breadcrumbs for coating fish, pork, and veal fillets before frying. It is an excellent herb in seafood sauces and cocktails, in lentil, pea and bean soups, and in soufflés. While being stimulating and pleasing to the taste buds savory is also an excellent substitute for pepper and other spices, which do not agree with some people. In cooking, savory and hyssop may often be interchanged.

SAVORY TEA
(1 cup)

To alleviate chest colds and to help digestion. Bring 250ml (8 fl oz) of water to the boil in a saucepan and add 1 teaspoon dried winter or summer savory, or 1 tablespoon of the fresh leaves, chopped. Cover and simmer for 1 minute. Turn the heat off and steep for several minutes longer. Strain and drink hot. Sweeten with a little honey if wished; a few drops of lemon juice may be added too.

SAVORY CHESTNUT SOUFFLÉ

(Serves 4)

A tasty dish for a light luncheon.

1 can unsweetened chestnut
purée
2 teaspoons finely grated onion
1 tablespoon finely chopped fresh
savory (or 2 teaspoons crumbled
or ground dried savory

salt to taste
4 eggs, separated

Put the chestnut purée into a bowl, and stir in the onion, savory and
salt. Beat the egg yolks and blend into the purée. Whip the whites
until stiff but not dry, then fold lightly and thoroughly into the
chestnut mixture. Turn into a buttered soufflé dish and bake in a
moderately hot oven (190°C, 375°F) for 30 to 35 minutes, when the
soufflé should be well risen and golden. Serve immediately.
Accompany with a tossed green salad and a jug of sorrel sauce
(page 32), or the savory yoghurt sauce given in the next recipe
(but omit the prawns).

FAMILY SOUP
(Serves 6)

1 lamb shank
200 g (8 oz) ham hocks
200 g (8 oz) stew beef, roughly cut up
1 carrot, diced
1 parsnip, diced
1 turnip, diced
2 stalks celery, chopped
2 onions, chopped
2 cloves garlic, peeled and left whole

200g (8 oz) brown beans
200 g (8 oz) lentils
salt to taste
a few black peppercorns
3 bay leaves
4 tablespoons chopped fresh savory tops (or 2 tablespoons crumbled or ground dried savory)

Put all the ingredients together in a soup pot with enough water to cover (about 5 litres or 4 quarts). Bring to the boil, turn the heat down and boil slowly for 2½ to 3 hours, skimming off any foam. Before serving, lift out the meat and bones. Ladle the hot soup into bowls and sprinkle with extra chopped savory.

PRAWNS IN SAVORY YOGHURT SAUCE
(Serves 2)

250ml (8 fl oz) natural (plain) yoghurt
1½ tablespoons tomato paste
2 good teaspoons finely chopped savory tops (or 1 teaspoon crumbled or ground dried savory)

a few drops soy sauce
200g (8 oz) prawns

Mix all the ingredients together except the prawns. Chill. Peel the prawns and fold into the sauce. Serve in individual glasses as for prawn cocktail. An excellent accompaniment is a small plate of thin brown bread sandwiches filled with chopped marjoram or chopped chervil or parsley.

GRETTA ANNA TEPLITZKY'S SEVEN BEAN SALAD WITH SAVORY

(Serves about 14)

My friend Gretta, a dynamic person and an inspired cooking teacher, devised this nourishing high-protein bean salad. It is an excellent standby for a cold buffet for about 14 people. Quantities may be halved for a lesser number of people.

3 tablespoons each of the following dried beans: kidney beans, cannelini beans, black-eyed peas, and navy beans
8 tablespoons dried lima beans
1 x 250g (10 oz) packet frozen lima beans (or a can of lima beans)
1 x 250g (10 oz) packet frozen fava beans (or a can of fava beans)

4 tablespoons finely chopped shallots
1 sweet red pepper, chopped
2 large cloves garlic, crushed
3 tablespoons finely chopped fresh parsley
3 tablespoons finely chopped fresh savory tops
plenty of salt and pepper
8 tablespoons vegetable oil
2½ tablespoons white vinegar

Cook together in salted water until tender—about 1½ hours—the dried kidney, cannelini, black-eyed peas and navy beans. Cook the dried lima beans separately because they will take a little longer. Let all the beans cool. Meanwhile cook both kinds of frozen beans according to the directions given on the packages (unless you are using canned beans instead, when they should be simply drained). Toss all the cooled beans well together with the rest of the ingredients listed above. Chill.

Thyme

The keen, savoury scent of thyme is familiar to us all. There are numerous kinds, all members of the Labiatae family: there are carpeting thymes, decorative variegated-leaved thymes and culinary thymes. The two most outstanding for use in cooking are the pungent grey-leaved garden thyme (*Thymus vulgaris*), and the more subtle lemon-scented thyme (*T. citriodorus*) whose smooth green leaves have a lemon fragrance. Both types bloom in spring and summer, the flowers ranging in hue from garden thyme's creamy-pink to lemon thyme's deeper shade of pink.

Thyme originally grew in Mediterranean countries, and it is truly at home on Greek hillsides—many say the scent of thyme growing there is more piercing than any other. Certainly honey gathered from Greek wild thyme is world-famous for its unique flavour, especially the honey from Mount Hymettus. Wherever thyme grows, as long as it is in the sun it absorbs light and warmth and converts these forces into volatile oils, giving the plant its rich perfume and health-giving substances. Because of this, thyme is valued for its ability to help cure colds and coughs, to aid digestion, to relieve cramp and colic, and to help dispel headaches and giddiness. It benefits children suffering from whooping-cough and loss of appetite, and helps promote sound sleep. Like sage, thyme has antiseptic qualities, and the name in its Greek form was a derivative of a word meaning 'to fumigate'. Others say the name comes from the Greek word *thumus*, signifying courage. In ancient days an infusion of thyme was given as a remedy for depression.

Oil of thyme is distilled from the fresh leaves and flowers of *T. vulgaris*. One of its chief elements is thymol, a powerful antiseptic, used extensively for its germicidal action.

Thyme goes with marjoram and sage into a mixed herb blend, and with marjoram, parsley and a bay-leaf it goes to make up a bouquet garni. It may also be used on its own in hearty meat dishes and with many vegetables. Try lemon thyme for a change when you wish for a more delicate flavour than that of garden thyme: it is particularly good with chicken and fish, and in omelettes.

When growing scented or variegated thymes, I have found the only sure way of having a plant true to type is to take cuttings, or to divide roots. You cannot be sure with seed. So for lemon thyme do this in spring and early summer. For garden thyme, which is not classed as a hybrid, sow seed in spring or autumn (or propagate by cuttings or root division if you prefer) and sow where the plants are to remain. Keep the ground moist until the green shoots appear, and make sure a sunny, well-drained position has been chosen.

Garden thyme is a shrubby plant growing to about 30cm (12 in) in height. Lemon thyme is smaller, with a spreading habit. Although these thymes are perennial, they need renewing every two years and should be cut back hard at the end of flowering.

For drying, follow the directions on page 126.

Thyme's aromatic qualities are said to help enliven flowers and vegetables growing nearby in the garden.

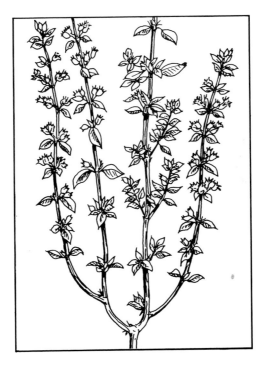

THYME FLAVOURED TRIPE
(Serves 2 or 3)

800g (2 lb) tripe
400g (1 lb) ripe tomatoes
salt to taste
2 branches garden thyme or
lemon thyme (or 1 teaspoon dried
thyme)

1 clove garlic, peeled and
chopped
Parmesan cheese, grated

Wash and clean the tripe. Cut it into fairly small dice, cover with water and bring to the boil. Simmer gently for 1 hour, then pour off the water. Meanwhile, make a purée of the tomatoes by removing the skins and stewing to a pulp with the salt. Measure the pulp—there should be about 315ml (10 fl oz) but if a little short add some water or stock. Pour the tomato purée on to the tripe in the saucepan, add the thyme and garlic and simmer for another hour. Remove the thyme branches, most of the leaves will have come off during cooking but if any remain, scrape them off into the saucepan using a spoon. Serve the tripe hot with a sprinkling of Parmesan cheese over each serving. Boiled brown rice and a crisp tossed salad make a good accompaniment to this dish.

THYME FLAVOURED GRILLED LAMB'S FRY

Skin one lamb's liver and cut it into slices. Brush one side of each slice with a mixture of 2 tablespoons vegetable oil, 1 teaspoon dried thyme, a crushed clove of garlic, and some salt and pepper. Place under the griller and cook, then turn the slices and brush with thyme-flavoured oil before completing the cooking. Serve with grilled bacon.

CARROT AND THYME SOUP

(Serves 5 or 6)   12-3-97

The tonic and digestive properties of thyme, together with vitamin C-rich carrots, tomatoes, paprika and lemon juice, make this a nourishing soup to help ward off winter colds.

200g (8 oz) carrots, coarsely grated
4 shallots, finely chopped
200g (8 oz) tomatoes, peeled and finely chopped
About 8 branches garden thyme or lemon thyme tied together (or 2 teaspoons dried thyme)

1 clove garlic, finely chopped
2 teaspoons paprika
1 tablespoon lemon juice
salt to taste
1.8 litres (3 pt) chicken stock

Put all the ingredients into a saucepan and simmer with the lid on for 30 minutes. Remove the thyme stalks (most of the leaves will have floated off during cooking) and serve with a sprinkling of parsley. In summer, for a jellied soup blend 2 tablespoons gelatine into some of the hot stock at the end of cooking, pour back into the soup, stir well and chill overnight.

THYME TEA

An old remedy for coughs, colds, catarrh, sore throats and flatulence. Pour 625ml (1 pt) boiling water over 25g (1 oz) dried thyme. Cover and infuse for 15 minutes. Strain and sweeten with honey. Take one or more tablespoons several times daily.
If making tea with the fresh herb, pick a bunch of garden thyme and put it in a saucepan with 625ml (1 pt) water. Cover and simmer for 20 minutes. Drain and use as above.

Chicory

Chicory (*Cichorium intybus*), a perennial belonging to the Compositae family, is also sometimes known as witloof or Belgian endive, which makes for some confusion. I have seen all three names on one label of imported canned chicory heads, which certainly does make identification easier, knowing that they are one and the same. Another name for this herb is succory.

The ancient world knew chicory: Arabian physicians used the plant, and the classical writers Horace, Virgil, Ovid and Pliny mention its use as a vegetable and in salads. It is thought by some scholars that the name succory came from the Latin *succurrere*, to run under, because of the depth of the roots. Another suggestion is that succory may be a corruption of chicory, or *cichorium*, a word of Egyptian origin.

Chicory is found growing wild in many parts of Europe. It is a stately herb reaching a height of 1.8 to 2.4m (6 to 8 ft). The lower leaves of the plant are broad and long like spinach leaves; as the stems lengthen, the leaves become much smaller and continue ever more sparsely almost to the top. The foliage has been used as a blue dye. Chicory greens make an excellent fodder for some animals, including sheep, cows and horses. We always had chicory growing near the top paddock for Hector, my son Ian's horse: a few leaves mixed with his feed, or handed to him over the fence, helped keep him in good condition. In spring, the stalks began to rise until they were 1.8m (6 ft) tall. When summer came, all the upper stems and branches exploded into a galaxy of pale heaven-blue flowers, like a burst of stars—the colour especially attracts the bumble bee. The circular blooms are nearly 5cm (2in) across, with rayed, tissue-thin petals finely serrated at the tips, and the frail stamens are almost navy blue. The flowers open only in the mornings and are closed by midday, except in dull weather, when they remain open all day: unfortunately, they do not last indoors.

When chicory is in flower, I think of it as succory, its old English name, and of an ancient legend that the succory of the fields was said to ensure fidelity in love, and that it was a favourite ingredient in love philtres.

Chicory taken in moderate quantities is a tonic herb, helping the functions of the liver and gall. The leaves are eaten raw or cooked. The root when roasted and ground is often used as an ingredient to mix with coffee, or is taken on its own as a beverage, especially suited to people suffering from bilious attacks. However, it is not supposed to be good for those who are anaemic. The flavour of the leaves varies in strength according to the method of cultivation. If the plants grow in a natural state in the garden, one or two young leaves are a sufficient addition to a salad, or to boil with spinach, for they are somewhat bitter. When growth is forced in the dark, the leaves are blanched, and both the flavour and texture become much more delicate.

For growing chicory in the garden as a useful addition to salads and to mix with cooked, leafy vegetables, sow seed in spring and autumn. Plants do well under almost any conditions, but prefer a certain amount of sunshine, good drainage, and water in dry weather. The leaves are not usually dried, but for teas they may be dried by laying them flat on sheets of paper, then store them whole, or crumble them into containers.

When treated as a vegetable, chicory is one of those herbs that comes into its own during the winter months. To achieve this, seed is sown in late spring, and blanching is carried out by lifting the roots about mid-autumn, when they are 7 to 9cm (3 to 3½ in) in diameter, after removing the big green tops. The roots are then packed upright, closely together, in boxes filled with approximately 12cm (5 in) of light soil, in a moist, dark place for several weeks. The new oncoming leaves become blanched and elongated, but if there is not enough darkness the heads may be green-tinted, which results in bitterness. As the tips of chicory begin to protrude through the soil they are ready for cutting.

Fresh, blanched chicory is available in winter from greengrocers' shops, and is recognized by its closely folded heads of pearly leaves—each head about 100g (4 oz). It is also seen in cans in grocery shops.

For eating blanched chicory raw, either cut the heads in quarters lengthwise and pour French dressing over, or tear to pieces and mix with other salad greens. For cooking, chicory may be steamed whole in butter, or cut into thick circles and steamed. It can be boiled in water for 10 minutes, drained, then served covered with melted butter or with white sauce and melted cheese.

BRAISED CHICORY WITH MARJORAM
(Serves 4)

The chicory must be of the best possible quality for this dish—the leaves white, without any trace of green. If necessary, drop the heads into boiling water first for a few minutes to help eliminate any bitterness.

400g (1 lb) chicory heads
butter (or margarine)

1 tablespoon chopped fresh marjoram leaves (or 2 teaspoons dried marjoram)
salt and pepper

Wash the chicory and trim it. Cut it into thick circles and pack into a buttered casserole dish with some marjoram, salt, pepper and pieces of butter between each layer. Put the lid on and bake in a moderate oven (150°C, 300°F) for 1¼ to 1½ hours. Serve hot.

CHICORY AND APPLE SALAD

This excellent salad is beneficial for the liver.

400g (1 lb) chicory heads
2 medium-size crisp apples
1 teaspoon aniseed (or dill or caraway seed)

French dressing (made with 3 tablespoons vegetable salad oil, 1 tablespoon lemon juice, salt and freshly ground pepper)

Wash and dry the chicory heads. Cut each into quarters, or slice them into thick circles. Peel and core the apples, and chop into cubes. Toss the chicory, aniseed and apple together with the dressing, adding extra salt and pepper if liked.

POACHED CHICORY
(Serves 4)

To serve as a vegetable.
Poach 400g (1 lb) chicory heads whole (or, if large, cut in half) in a pan of water with a dash of either lemon juice, white wine or white vinegar, and a bay-leaf, some salt and a few peppercorns. Cook until the heads are tender—20 to 30 minutes. Drain, and arrange on a serving dish. Mask with béchamel sauce, hollandaise sauce or melted butter, and sprinkle with finely chopped green dill.

Comfrey

Comfrey (*Symphytum officinale*) belongs to the Boraginaceae family and is native to Europe and parts of Asia. There are several types, the best known being the *officinale* grown by the medieval monks in their physic gardens.

Comfrey has a variety of medicinal uses, and was once valued as a wound-healer and as a remedy for broken bones (hence the popular country names of Knitbone or Boneset), also as an expectorant for catarrhal congestion. Owing to the great amount of mucilage—a glutinous substance—in its composition, comfrey has also been used to soothe intestinal troubles and lung complaints: the root is more effective than the leaves for this.

As external remedies comfrey leaves are esteemed in the form of fomentations for sprains and bruises, and poultices for severe cuts, abscesses and ulcers. Comfrey foliage also has a good reputation as fodder for most animals.

Young comfrey leaves are pleasant to eat. The older leaves are too coarse in texture, and rather strong in flavour. The new leaves make an excellent, healthful vegetable and help to promote good circulation. Dried comfrey leaves should be kept as a standby to make into a tea for bronchitis and colds during winter.

Comfrey likes a shady place in the garden, although it will grow anywhere. Sow seed in spring or autumn, or propagate by root division at these times. Once in the garden it is almost impossible to eliminate owing to the persistence of its deeply penetrating roots: any little piece of root that is broken during digging—and left there—will shoot. The plant is an evergreen and may be picked throughout winter; by summer it will have grown in height and especially in breadth, to grand proportions, and must be kept in check. The outside lower leaves may be 60cm (24 in) long and 20cm (8 in) across, and when in bloom the plant grows to 1.2m (4 ft) tall. Like borage, the leaves have a rough texture and a sticky feel. The lavender-coloured flowers appear during summer: they are bell-shaped and grow in clusters.

To harvest the leaves for drying, pick them before midday and spread them flat on racks or paper in a shady, airy place. When brittle, crumble them coarsely and pack into airtight containers.

COMFREY FRITTERS

Comfrey fritters . . . are among the less eccentric of 'wild foods'. A Comfrey leaf seems unpromising; rough if not tough. All you do is strip the leaves off the plant, dip them first in cold water, then in batter: after which you transfer them to a frying pan on the sizzle. They emerge like green and golden fish. And the trouble is how to stop eating them. The recipe is German.

GEOFFREY GRIGSON A Herbal of All Sorts

COMFREY PUMPKIN TART
(Serves 6)

Pastry
125g (5 oz) unbleached flour
125g (5 oz) wheatgerm
salt to taste
100g (4 oz) butter or margarine
2 or 3 tablespoons iced water

Filling
400g (1 lb) pumpkin, peeled and
cut up

a knob of butter
1 teaspoon honey
salt to taste
1 tablespoon kelp granules
90g (3½ oz) finely shredded
young comfrey leaves
1 tablespoon grated onion
125ml (4 fl oz) milk
1 egg, separated

The pastry Stir the flour, wheatgerm and salt together, then rub in the
butter or margarine until the mixture resembles breadcrumbs. Add
the water gradually and knead the dough. Take a 25cm (10 in) pie-
plate and rub it over with butter. Roll the dough out to the same size
and line the plate with it. Trim the edges, prick
well all over and bake in a moderate oven (175°C, 350°F) until
cooked—20 to 30 minutes.
The filling Boil the pumpkin in salted water until cooked. Drain, then
mash smoothly with the butter (or vegetable margarine). Beat in the
honey, salt, kelp, comfrey, grated onion, milk and egg yolk. Whip the
egg white until stiff and fold into the mixture, spread lightly on to the
tart shell and return it to a hot oven (240°C, 450°F) for 5 to 7
minutes. Serve hot or cold with a tossed green salad.

COMFREY TEA

A remedy for coughs and chest colds. Allow 25g (1 oz) dried leaves to 625ml (1 pt) boiling water. Pour the water over the leaves, cover and allow to stand for 30 minutes. Strain the liquid and use. Drink 1 cup two or three times a day, sweetened with honey if wished.

Garlic

Garlic (*Allium sativum*) belongs with onions and chives to the Liliaceae family. It is thought to have originated in south-western Siberia, whence it spread to southern Europe. The value of garlic does not lie in the foliage but in the bulbs, which grow underground. Each bulb is made up of small segments covered by a papery, pearly skin (these are called cloves).

Garlic was included in the diet of the ancient Egyptians and it also had a meaning in the ceremonial taking of oaths. It was widely eaten by the early Romans and Greeks, some of whom had mixed feelings about it. Horace deplored the eating of garlic; and those who had partaken of the pungent bulb were not allowed to enter the temples of Cybele. Homer had more respect for it, and recounts how, owing to the virtues of garlic, Ulysses escaped from the enchantress Circe.

Garlic has been known for centuries to contain antiseptic substances, and is particularly good for the intestines. The eating of garlic cloves is recommended to help lower high blood-pressure to expel worms, and to ward off colds as well as assisting in curing them. It acts on the kidneys, induces perspiration and is an expectorant. Syrup of garlic is helpful to sufferers from chest congestion, especially those with bronchitis. The bruised bulbs mixed with lard and rubbed on the chest have relieved whooping-cough sufferers. A clove or two is even good for rheumatism when pounded and mixed with honey and taken regularly for two or three nights.

This potent bulb has a reputation for clearing the complexion if taken intensively for a few days, which was proved to us one weekend when one of our sons took garlic with every meal (also in between) using it sliced with tomatoes on buttered biscuits. He chose to do this when most of the family was away, and by Monday his teenage skin was quite unblemished!

During World War I the raw juice of garlic was put on sterilized swabs and applied to wounds to prevent them from turning septic. Garlic has also been included in antiseptic ointments and lotions. One of its early uses was in the treatment of leprosy. It was one of the main herbs used in the famous Four Thieves Vinegar as a protection against the plague. The story goes that in the terrible pestilence that swept Marseilles in 1722, claiming many victims, four thieves robbed the bodies of the dead without catching the disease. They later confessed that they had liberally splashed on themselves an aromatic vinegar which included in its composition the tops of wormwood, rosemary, sage, mint, rue, lavender flowers, cinnamon, cloves, nutmeg and a plentiful amount of garlic. These ingredients are infused in red wine vinegar in the sun for a month, then strained, and the vinegar kept in a tightly corked bottle.

Use garlic in cooking, not only for its unique, penetrating, savoury flavour, but because it helps the digestion, being said to keep the lining of the stomach in good condition. Garlic pills are available commercially today. Many recipes include a clove or two of garlic but if you do not like the taste and smell at first, try rubbing a single cut clove around the saucepan or salad bowl, then gradually use more. Cloves of garlic can go into soups, meat or vegetable casseroles, and many meat dishes. Mashed into butter, as a garlic spread, it makes delicious garlic bread. One of garlic's most famous uses is in the pungent French sauce aioli (*ail* is the French word for garlic). This sauce is made with peeled garlic first pounded to a cream and then mixed with egg yolks, olive oil then being gradually stirred in until the mixture is thick and golden. Elizabeth David says a true aioli should be a smooth mayonnaise with a powerful garlic flavour which tingles in the throat as it is swallowed.

Garlic is easy to grow. It flourishes in a sunny position and in most types of soil, doing best in rich, sandy loam. It is planted in spring and autumn. Each knob is divided into separate cloves, the outer ones being the most suitable for planting. Push them into 5cm (2 in) drills, 15cm (6 in) apart, cover with soil and firm down. Keep the bed weeded, and water in dry weather. The long grey-green stalks and spiky leaves shoot up quickly, the stems carrying showy heads of pincushion-like blooms resembling enormous, faded chive flowers. These are sometimes used for cut flowers. The bulbs are ready for lifting about 5 to 6 months after planting, when the flowers begin to fall and the whole plant starts withering. Dig up the bulbs, shake them free of dirt, cut off the dead leaves, and hang them by their shrivelled stalks in an airy place to dry out thoroughly and harden.

Dehydrated garlic is packaged commercially. The cloves are peeled of their fine skin and sliced into flakes, then dried. The result is very pungent, and only a small amount should be used in place of fresh garlic. Garlic powder is also available, but this does not have the same strength as the flakes. Garlic salt is a blend of garlic powder and salt.

In the garden, garlic and roses benefit each other. Garlic also contributes in maintaining the health of stone-fruit trees. Pieces of garlic scattered amongst grain helps to keep weevils away.

AIOLI

Particularly nice when served with fish, whole boiled or baked potatoes, beetroot, hard-boiled eggs, globe artichokes, steamed chicken or boiled beef.

12 garlic cloves, peeled	435ml (14 fl oz) best olive oil
salt	a few drops lemon juice
3 egg yolks	

Mash the garlic cloves to a cream on a board with a little salt, using a sharp knife, then transfer to a bowl. Stir in the egg yolks with a wooden spoon, and when well blended start beating in the oil drop by drop. As the mixture thickens, and when about half the oil has been used, add the rest of the oil a little more quickly, in a steady stream, still beating. Add the lemon juice last. If the aioli separates—and this applies to any mayonnaise—put a fresh yolk in another bowl and slowly add the curdled sauce to it.

LINIMENT FOR BRONCHITIS

An old remedy for bronchitis and tightness of the chest.

Chop up a clove of garlic and mix it into a jar of Vaseline. Stand the jar in a warm place (for example, at the back of the stove) for a few days. Remove. When it is cold, massage a little into the back and chest at intervals.

GARLIC BUTTER

This spread is for garlic bread, or can be used as a filling for snails (escargots) in the shell. Put in a bowl 120g (5 oz) softened butter or good vegetable margarine. Take 1 large clove of garlic (or 2 small ones), peel it, place on a board with a little salt, and with the point of a sharp knife chop and crush the garlic. (The salt helps with the pulverizing.) Mash the butter and garlic together and let the mixture stand for 30 minutes before using.

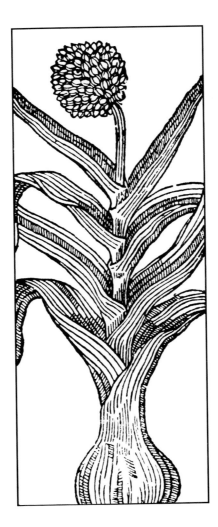

SYRUP OF GARLIC

An old recipe to relieve coughs and colds.

Pour 1.25l (1 qrt) boiling water over 400g (1 lb) cut-up garlic cloves.
Cover and leave for 12 hours. Strain, then stir enough sugar into the
liquid to make a syrup. (The garlic water may be gently heated to
quickly dissolve the sugar.) A little vinegar added to the syrup helps
to tone down the strong odour.

TASTY BROWN GARLIC RICE
(Serves 4)

*Dr Vogel, the celebrated naturopath, advocates brown rice for helping to
reduce high blood-pressure. He says unpolished whole or brown rice
contains nine and a half times more minerals than the polished kind. When
cooking brown rice, use only as much water as the rice needs to become
soft. When the rice is cooked and dry, stir some finely chopped garlic into it,
and some green herbs as well if you like. Do not add salt.*

625ml (1 pt) water
200g (8 oz) brown rice
1 teaspoon finely chopped garlic

1 tablespoon finely chopped
marjoram

Bring the water to the boil in a saucepan. Add the rice (wash only if
dusty), put the lid on, and boil gently until the water has been
absorbed—about 40 minutes. With a fork stir in the garlic and
marjoram, and serve at once.

Horseradish

Pungent horseradish (*Cochlearia armoracia*) has never lost its popularity. It belongs to the Cruciferae family, being a cousin to mustard and cress, and in common with the other members of the family it is permeated with etheric oils rich in sulphur. Crucifers are identified by their flowers, which are composed of four petals in the shape of a Greek cross; among all the two thousand and more species in the family there are no plants that are poisonous.

Although horseradish has been cultivated since earliest times, its origins are obscure. Some say it first grew in Eastern Europe, from the Caspian shores through Russia and Poland to Finland. It is thought to have been one of the bitter herbs eaten at the feast of the Passover, the others being coriander, horehound, lettuce and nettle.

During the Middle Ages both the leaves and roots of horseradish were used in medicine and as a condiment. In recent years, mainly the root has been used, although the tender young leaves may be chopped finely and mixed into salads.

The piercing flavour of horseradish root is said to help enliven a lazy metabolism, and assists in relieving congestion in liver and gall. It has antiseptic and stimulant properties, is slightly laxative, helps the kidneys, is an expectorant, and is excellent when mixed with oil and used as a rub for chest congestion. Once, when suffering from a stubborn chest cold, I was given a treatment of extract of horseradish and avocado oil which had been made into an ointment. Its curative effect was amazing.

Horseradish acts on the digestion when taken with rich and oily foods. It is held that mixing a little grated horseradish with salads regularly will reduce one's susceptibility to catching colds and chills, and helps get rid of persistent coughs. For older people, it is believed to help regenerate the blood-vessels and reduce blood-pressure.

For an effective skin-refresher infuse some of the sliced root in milk, and pat the milk on the skin. Also, juice from the root when mixed with white vinegar and patted on the skin will help fade freckles. A weak solution was formerly much used as a drink to remedy worms in children.

In food, the root is grated and combined with other ingredients to make horseradish sauce, that well-known accompaniment to meats. Fresh horseradish roots are not easily available unless you grow them yourself, but there is an excellent substitute in dried horseradish commercially prepared in the form of small grains, which reconstitute and swell in a moist component, giving a good texture. This is more satisfactory than powdered dried horseradish, which has no texture and is much weaker in flavour than the grains. A pinch of freshly grated or dried granulated horseradish gives a pungent bite to seafood sauces, sour cream dressing for salads and baked potatoes, savoury butters, mayonnaise, vegetable juices, dips and spreads.

Horseradish does not usually set seed but is propagated from roots or root cuttings, which are very hardy and persistent. If unchecked, the plant easily becomes a pest. For top-quality flavoured roots the best soil is sandy loam which has been deeply dug over; the ground should be kept fairly moist and well drained. Treat plants as annuals, lifting the roots and replanting every year. When lifted, roots may be stored in dry sand and used as required.

In the garden, horseradish helps to make potato plants more healthy and disease-resistant.

HORSERADISH SAUCE

Here are two recipes for sauces to accompany roast or boiled beef or pork, cold cooked fish, or boiled mutton.

Sauce 1 Whip 150ml (5 fl oz) cream until thickened. Stir in
2 teaspoons white vinegar, 1 teaspoon mustard powder (or
½ teaspoon prepared mustard), salt to taste, 1 teaspoon raw sugar and
2 tablespoons grated fresh horseradish or bottled grated horseradish.
Leave for at least 30 minutes
before using.
Sauce 2 To 250ml (8 fl oz) white or béchamel sauce add 2
tablespoons grated fresh horseradish or bottled grated horseradish, a
dash of mustard powder or prepared mustard, a pinch each of salt and
sugar, 2 teaspoons lemon juice and 1 tablespoon cream. Stir well
together and leave for 30 minutes or more before using. Serve cold,
or heat gently and serve hot.

APPLE HORSERADISH CREAM

Peel and grate 2 apples, mix with 2 tablespoons fresh grated
horseradish or bottled grated horseradish, toss with the juice of 1
lemon, salt to taste, 1 teaspoon sugar, and 2 teaspoons chopped mint.
Fold into 300g sour cream. Use as a dressing for peeled chopped
avocado, peeled chopped cucumber, or cooked
diced beetroot.

FROZEN HORSERADISH CREAM

150ml (5 fl oz) heavy cream
2 tablespoons freshly grated
horseradish or bottled grated
horseradish

a squeeze of lemon juice
a pinch of salt
2 teaspoons finely chopped
parsley

Mix all the ingredients together and pour into a shallow dish. Freeze.
Cut the frozen horseradish cream into squares, arrange in a chilled
dish, and serve with cold meat or fish.

HORSERADISH BREAD SAUCE

Excellent with roast turkey, duck or goose, roast beef, or boiled corned beef.

375ml (12 fl oz) milk
4 tablespoons grated fresh
horseradish or bottled grated
horseradish
3 tablespoons soft breadcrumbs

1 tablespoon butter or table
margarine
1 teaspoon lemon juice
salt to taste

Soak the milk, horseradish and breadcrumbs in a saucepan for 20 minutes, then bring very slowly to simmering point and turn the heat off immediately. Stir in the butter, lemon juice and salt. Cover the saucepan and stand it at the back of the stove until ready to serve.

HORSERADISH BUTTER

Put 60g (2½ oz) butter or margarine into a bowl and soften. Add 1 tablespoon freshly grated horseradish, or bottled grated horseradish, and mash together. Cover and chill for at least 30 minutes. Serve with grilled meat, fish or poultry.

TO RELIEVE A HEAVY COLD

An old recipe from *Lotions and Potions:* grate horseradish and inhale the fumes that arise.

Horehound

Recently a much wider interest than before has been shown in the herb horehound (*Marrubium vulgare*), which is the white-flowering horehound and a member of the Labiatae family. The name is mostly associated with horehound beer, a popular non-alcoholic beverage. The herb is said to be indigenous to Britain. It grows freely in Europe, Asia and North Africa, and the Romans esteemed it highly. Some historical writers say it was one of the bitter herbs eaten by the Hebrews at the Feast of the Passover. The generic name is derived from the Hebrew *marrob*, a bitter juice. The Egyptian priests knew horehound and called it Seed of Horus or Bull's Blood. It was an ingredient of antidotes for some types of poison. In *Gardens of Delight* Eleanour Sinclair Rohde relates that a ninth-century monk wrote of it: 'Horehound is bitter to the palate, yet its scent is sweet. Drink horehound hot from the fire if you are poisoned by your stepmother.'

Black horehound (*Ballota nigra*) also of the Labiatae family, is distinguished from the white by its taller growth, its unpleasant smell, and the purple colour of the flowers. Although shunned because of its odour, black horehound has been used in the past as an antidote for the bite of a mad dog's 'venom'd tooth'. The generic name, *Ballota*, is derived from the Greek, meaning rejection.

White horehound has been valued for centuries in treating colds, and early herbals give detailed instructions for making syrups and infusions of horehound to take for coughs and 'wheezing of the lungs'. Culpeper says that when horehound is taken with the roots of orris it 'helpeth to expectorate tough phlegm from the chest'. It is still considered effective as an expectorant, as well as having tonic and mildly laxative properties, and may be taken as a syrup, a tea, a gargle, or made into candy. As an insect repellant, horehound steeped in milk and placed in a fly-infested area is said to make the flies disappear.

White horehound is a branching shrubby herb growing to about 30cm (12 in) in height. The rather fleshy leaves are crinkled with numerous tiny veins, and are a soft greyish-green colour. The scent is both sharp and sweet, the flavour bitter. In summer the small white whorls of flowers appear at intervals in dense clusters on either side of the stems, seeming to encircle them, and the plant stays in bloom for months. It is a tough little plant, and thrives in poor, dry soil in a sunny position. Propagation is by root division or cuttings taken in spring: seed may be sown in spring and autumn.

To dry white horehound, pick stalks of flowers and leaves just as the plant begins to bloom, and before midday, and hang in bunches in an airy place. When dry, crumble off the leaves and flowers, and break up the brittle stalks, which have value as well. Store in airtight containers.

HOREHOUND TEA
(1 cup)

A remedy for a cold. Pour 1 cup boiling water over 1 teaspoon dried leaves (or 2 or 3 fresh leaves). Cover and infuse for several minutes, then strain. The taste is bitter, so flavour with lemon juice and sweeten with honey. Take three times a day.

HOREHOUND CANDY

Pour 1.25 litres (2 pt) boiling water over 25g (1 oz) dried horehound. Cover and infuse for 30 minutes. Strain well through gauze or cheesecloth, pressing out every vestige of juice from the herb. Measure the liquid into a saucepan, and for every 2 cups horehound tea add 3 cups brown sugar and 1 teaspoon cream of tartar. Warm the mixture to dissolve the sugar, then bring to the boil and continue boiling until a little of the toffee hardens in cold water. Have a buttered dish ready and pour the horehound candy into it (or fill individual paper cases with candy). Mark into squares and allow it to set.

Book List

The books marked with an asterisk were particularly valuable in the research for my book. —R.H.

Back, Edward, *The Twelve Healers*. C. W. Daniel Co Ltd, England, 1964.

Bardswell, Frances A., *The Herb Garden*. Adam & Charles Black, London, 1911.

Coates, Peter, *Roses*. Weidenfeld & Nicolson, London, 1962.

Coronation Cookery Book, 6th edition, 1951. Compiled for Country Women's Association of New South Wales by Jessie Sawyer and Sara Moore-Sims.

Culpeper, Nicholas, *Culpeper's Complete Herbal*. W. Foulsham & Co Ltd, London.

David, Elizabeth, *French Provincial Cooking*. Penguin Books, Harmondsworth, 1964.

David, Elizabeth, *Spices, Salt and Aromatics in the English Kitchen*, Penguin Books, Harmondsworth, 1970.

*Geuter, Maria, *Herbs in Nutrition*. Bio-Dynamic Agricultural Association, London, 1962.

*Grieve, Mrs M., *A Modern Herbal*. 2 vols. Edited by Mrs C. F. Leyel. Hafner Publishing Co., New York, 1959.

Grigson, Geoffrey, *A Herbal of All Sorts*. Phoenix House, London, 1959.

Hauschka, Rudolph, *Nutrition*. Stuart & Watkins, London, 1967.

Heath, Ambrose, *Home-made Wines and Liqueurs*. Herbert Jenkins, London, 1953.

Heaton, Nell, *A Calendar of Country Receipts*. Faber & Faber, London.

Hemphill, Rosemary, *Herbs and Spices*. Penguin Books, Harmondsworth, 1966.

Janes, E. R., *Growing Vegetables for Show*. Penguin Books, Harmondsworth, 1956.

Leyel, Mrs C. F., *The Truth About Herbs*. Culpeper Press, London, 1954.

Leyel, Mrs C. F., and Hartley, Olga, *The Gentle Art of Cookery*. Chatto & Windus, London, 1925.

Loewenfeld, Claire, *Herb Gardening*. Garden Book Club, London, 1964.

Loewenfeld, Claire, and Back, Philippa, *Herbs for Health and Cookery*. Pan Books, London, 1965.

Lotions and Potions. Compiled by National Federation of Women's Institutes, England, 1956, and printed by Novello & Co. Ltd.

Miloradovich, Milo, *The Art of Cooking with Herbs and Spices*. Doubleday & Co., Inc., New York, 1950.

Moloney, Ted, and Coleman, Deke, *Oh, For a French Wife!* Shepherd Press, 1953.

*Philbrick, Helen, and Gregg, Richard B., *Companion Plants*. Stuart & Watkins, London, 1967.

Ranson, Florence, *British Herbs*. Penguin Books, Harmondsworth, 1949.

Rohde, Eleanour Sinclair, *A Garden of Herbs*. Medici Society, London.

Rohde, Eleanour Sinclair, *Herbs and Herb Gardening*. Medici Society, London, 1936.

Rohde, Eleanour Sinclair, *Shakespeare's Wild Flowers*. Medici Society, London, 1963.

Rohde, Eleanour Sinclair, *The Scented Garden*. Medici Society, London.

Rose Catalogue 1970. Roy H. Rumsey Pty Ltd, Dural, NSW.

Spry, Constance, and Hume, Rosemary, *The Constance Spry Cookery Book*. Reprint Society, London, 1958.

Stebbing, Lionel, *Honey as Healer*. Emerson Press, London, 1963.

Swane's Nursery Catalogue. Swane Bros Pty Ltd, Dural, N.S.W.

Vogel, Dr A., *The Nature Doctor*. Bioforce-Verlag, Teufen, Switzerland, 1952.

Walling, Edna, *A Gardener's Log*. Oxford University Press, London, 1948.

Webster, Helen Noyes, *Herbs*. Charles T. Branford Co., Boston, 1947.

Index

Nasturtium, 52, 66–67
  and peanut soup, 68
  salad, 67
Nasturtium officinale. See Watercress
Nepeta spp., 139
Nettle tops, in soups, 63

Oats, rolled, in Swiss breakfast, 77
Ocimum spp. *See* Basil
Oil: lavender, 43
  of thyme, 166
Ointment, elderflower, 89
Omelette, sorrel, 33
Oranges, compôte of, 77
Oregano, 138, 144–145
  dumplings, 148
  in moussaka, 152
  in zucchini salad, 151
Origanum dictamnus, 145
  marjorana. See Marjoram *vulgare.*
    See Oregano
Orris powder, 34
  in 'perfumed basket', 36
  in pot-pourri, 34, 40
  rinse, 36
  sachet, 36
Oswego tea, 58

Parsley, 2, 11–12
  in tabbouleh, 13
  jelly, 13
  tea, 14
  See also Bouquet garni
Paste, chervil, 7
Peanut and nasturtium soup, 68
Pennyroyal, 73
Pepper herb. *See* Savory
Peppermint, Mitcham, 73
  tea from, 73
'Perfumed basket', 36
Pest repellents, 44, 67, 85, 100, 101,
  158, 162, 180, 188
Petroselinum spp. *See* Parsley
Pimpinella anisum. See Anise;
  Aniseed
Polenta, 126
Pomander: apple, 103, 106
  kumquat, 110
Pot herbs, 3, 20–33

See also Borage; Dandelion
Pot-pourri, 40, 45
Potato caraway cream, 124
Poterium sanguisorba. See Salad
  burnet
Prawns: in yoghurt sauce, 164
  jellied, with cucumber and dill,
  132
Prunes, vanilla, in wine, 88
Pumpkin: and comfrey tart, 176
  and dill-seed soup, 130
Pungent herbs, 138, 139, 140–169
  See also individual herbs
Pyrus malus. See Crabapples

Quick protein lunch, 141
Quinces, 98, 111
  jelly from, 113

Restorative and tonic herbs,
  170–189
Rice, brown: and dill-seed salad, 130
  cooking of, 182
  tasty garlic, 182
Rice pudding, lemon verbena, 95
Rinse, clothes, 36
Rob, elderberry, 89
Rocket (roquette), 64
Rosa centifolia musoosa, 39
  gallica officinalis, 39
Rose-geranium leaves, in pot-pourri, 40
Rose-hip jelly, 114–115
  syrup, 115
Rose-hips, 98, 114
  and apple cheese, 116
  and apple snow, 117
Rose petal
  sandwiches, 41
  vinegar, 41
Rose petals, 39
  crystallized, 42
  in pot-pourri, 40
Rosemary, 138, 153–155
  and lima bean salad, 156
  and eggplant casserole, 155
  hair lotion, 153
  in herbed drumsticks, 156
  tea, 154, 156
  wine, 154, 155

Spicy fruit cake, 120–121
Spreads: cheese-ball, 10
  chervil, 7
  garlic, 179, 181
  horseradish, 185, 186
Steak and kidney casserole, with
  oregano dumplings, 148
Succory. *See* Chicory
Sunflower-seed cheese ball, 10
Swiss breakfast, with mint or balm, 77
Symphytum officinale. See Comfrey
Syrup: of garlic, 182
  of violets, 50
  rose-hip, 115

Tabbouleh, 13
Tanacetum vulgare. See Tansy
Tansy, 100
Taraxacum officinale. See Dandelion
Tarragon, 2, 15–16
  fish mould, 16
  vinegar, 17
  See also Fines herbes
Tart: apple and elderberry, 90
  sorrel juice, 31
  comfrey and pumpkin, 176
Tasty brown garlic rice, 182
Tea: aniseed, 119, 120
  balm, 76
  bergamot, 59
  borage, 26
  caraway seed, 120, 124
  comfrey, 177
  cooling ideas for, 78
  dandelion, 23
  dill-seed, 131
  elderflower, 87
  fennel-seed, 134
  horehound, 189
  hyssop, 142
  lemon verbena, 95
  lovage, 28
  marjoram, 148
  mint or balm in, 76
  mixed seed, 120
  Oswego, 58
  parsley, 14
  peppermint, 73
  rosemary, 154, 156

sage, 158
savory, 162
thyme, 169
violet-flower, 49
violet-leaf, 50
Teucrium marum, 139
Thyme, 138, 166–167
  and carrot soup, 169
  lamb's fry flavoured with, 168
  oil of, 166
  tea, 169
  tripe flavoured with, 168
  See also Bouquet garni; Cat-thyme;
  Lemon thyme; Mixed herbs
Thymus spp. *See* Thyme
Tomato sauce, 150
Tomatoes, baked eggs in, 57
Tonics: hair, 153, 160
  rosemary wine, 155
  See also Restorative and tonic herbs
Tripe, thyme-flavoured, 168
Tropaeolum majus. See Nasturtium
Tuna,
  mould of, with basil, 56

Vanilla prunes in wine, 88
Verbena, lemon. *See* Lemon verbena
Verbena officinalis, 93
Vervain, 93
Vesper-flower. *See* Rocket
Vinegar: elderflower, 85
  four-herbs, 56
  Four Thieves, 179
  rose petal, 41
  tarragon, 17
  violet, 47
Viola odorata. See Violets
Violet ice cream, 48
  milk, 49
  powder. *See* Orris powder
  tea, 49
  vinegar, 47
Violets, 47–48
  crystallized, 49
  dame's. *See* Rocket
  infusion of leaves of, 50
  leaves of, in soup, 63
  salad of leaves of, 50
  syrup of, 50

The Author

Rosemary Hemphill's love for plants and flowers began in her childhood in England where she spent happy years roaming the beautiful garden of her grandparents. This background, and her interest in history, were no doubt reponsible for the specialisation in growing culinary herbs that the Hemphills—Rosemary and her husband John—have been engaged in since 1957. They grew herbs at Somerset Cottage, Dural, a rural district outside Sydney, where interest in the project was widespread and immediate. Soon, the Hemphills were holding lecture days and blending their own herbs and spices commercially. This interest in herbs ranges from history and herb lore to the growing and drying of herbs and making of pot-pourri, and in the intervening years Rosemary has had more time to write and to ponder on the beauty of herbs and gardens: her books are very succesful and have been printed again and again, beginning with this classic text. As well as writing books about herbs, Rosemary Hemphill has contributed many articles on the subject to magazines such as *Vogue Living* and *House and Garden*.